WHEN COMEDIANS BECAME OUR INTELLECTUALS AND PROPHETS...

America!
Wake the *@$# Up!!!

A RETURN TO COMMON SENSE

R.A. Hviding

Dedication:

To my best friend and lover – my beautiful wife. A brilliant light in my darkest hour. If we ever find out love is a quantifiable force that reaches beyond time and space, you'll discover mine for you is eternal and immense.

Contents

Introduction

An interesting synthesis of thoughts has been occurring over the past number of years. Comedians have become the new intellectuals in society. Of course not all comedians, idiots are everywhere. However, there is a growing number of comedians who are flexing their intellectual muscles via various digital media platforms making their voices heard. In a country founded by intellectuals, ran by greedy idiots, comedians are becoming some of the loudest intellectual voices in the room. The country seems to be run by clowns. I'm not talking about good clowns, I'm talking about creepy John Wayne Gacy type clowns. Just look at the 2016 Presidential race! Out of 320 million people, the best we can fucking do is Hillary Clinton and Donald Trump? A real estate mogul/reality TV star vs. a criminal? At this rate, it's going to be Lindsey Lohan vs. the "Situation" from Jersey Shore by the next election cycle. The best summation of presidential political spectacle is from the election episode of South Park.

"No Matter Who You Vote For, It's Always between a Giant Douche and a Turd Sandwich!"- South Park

We all laugh because it's the truth, but what we really should be is pissed. It's that way by design. We should be pissed at the current state of our country, and what it has become. We should be pissed at what the future holds for our children and grandchildren. We should be pissed because we are getting fucked out of the American Dream. We live in a country where almost nobody actually owns anything. It's not yours unless the title of ownership is in your hot little hand. We are population where 60% of Americans have less than $1000 in their checking accounts. The young are yoked with student debt when they just are starting life. We have become dumbed down wage slaves who identify with freedom because we get to buy trinkets and we are told we are free, but we are far from free.

If lady liberty is a symbolic representation of our country, what would she look like? Well folks, she looks like a strung out crazy whore. She's in massive debt to loan sharks bankers who own her. A high percentage of what her children produces is stolen. She's always poking her nose in other people's business and causing violence. She's suspicious of her kids and is electronically spying on them. She doesn't teach her kids how to be independent thinkers, but dependent on her and subsequently on those who exploit her. Her children turn to those who have created the problems to fix their problems. Every decision she makes empowers her corporate owned pimps regardless of the negative impact on those she professes to love. Her children are so utterly brainwashed they don't understand their consent has been manufactured for decades. She does some really horrible shit, but has her children convinced it's for their own good. She gives her kids stupid shit to occupy themselves while colluding with her corporate pimps to create different ways to keep exploiting her children.

Lady Liberty needs an intervention soon, she is dying at the hands of the corporate oligarchy. What is the logical outcome if we keep heading in this insane direction? Does it make any sense to keep making ever increasing laws, regulations, and spending when the perceived "solutions" ultimately give more power and wealth to the people who created the problems in the first place? Or does it make more fucking sense to sever the relationship the corporate pimps have with Lady Liberty?

"We now live in a nation where doctors destroy health, lawyers destroy justice, universities destroy knowledge, the press destroys

information, religion destroys morals, and banks destroy the economy." -Chris Hedges

Before we get into the mix of deconstructing how we got to this point in history, a few words about me, the author. I studied and received degrees from a well know university in Political Science and Russian. I worked in finance for handful of years. I quickly figured out I didn't enjoy ripping people off for a living, and went into the blue collar world of being an electrician. I know, quite the career jump, but it was something honest.

It's very satisfying to create something or fix something and see it work. I've been a small business owner, I'm a father, and a husband. I've always been a student of history, an arm chair political scientist, and a guy who likes working with his hands. I've been student of philosophy for years because of an insatiable hunger to know how the world works. I want to know how things work. There is very little, if anything, I find problematic or uncomfortable to the extent I don't want to know about it or hear about it. If something is real, well documented, or ever rumored I want to explore the claim. I'll listen, then research, and give appropriate weight depending on the evidence when developing a certain view point. If the weight of evidence is presented forces me to change a view point, great. That means you are learning something new.

Over the years, I've become fearful of the direction we are heading. So, I took the last couple months to write this book. I have no fancy connections for editors, or publishers so please excuse any errors in formatting or grammar you may find. The point of this book is the message and ideas which need to resonant among thinking people regardless of religion, race, or political affiliation. We must provoke thought now, or more thinking will be done for us at our detriment. Even though it may be a longshot, I hope these

4

words will be read by some of the big mouth comedians we all love. A real message for change will ripple through our collective psyche, there is a much better way.

My approach to political philosophy and history is the same basic no nonsense approach I take when building and troubling shooting complicated electrical systems. Both worlds of politics and electricity function according to the same universal principle of causality, there is rhyme and reason in everything. In fact, the universe would not exist if it were not for causality. Like it or not we are all subject to this universal law. The only reason something may seem without rhyme or reason is due to missing information or information we refuse to consider because we don't like the causal condition which produced the effect. Think of the drug addict whose life is a mess, the last thing he will do is blame the drugs as a causal factor in destruction of his life. He'll blame everything that moves as the cause of his problems. If the truth is realized, objective and subjective reality slam into each other with enough force a realization of a need for change is created. No more living in fairytale land. No more running away from problems with mental gymnastics. Eventually, what is going on in our country will catch up to you or somebody you love.

The Principle of Causality with electricity is fairly simple, cause and effect is called line and load, or input and output. In politics it's much more complicated due to the sheer volume of bullshit wired into the system. However, things clear up in a hurry when you identify the people and follow the money and influence.

When an electrical system malfunctions we systematically go through the system by the means of a practical hands on methodology in terms of causality, and identify what mechanisms are broken or worn out. Normally there is little debate whether a mechanism within the system is broken or worn out, it's self-evident.

5

The only time when reality or truth of the problem gets obfuscated is when somebody's ego or money is part of the equation. Isn't it interesting how hard it is for people to accept the truth when the truth undermines their security, money, or ego? We see this manifest all the time when we wonder to ourselves, is this person stupid, a lair, or delusional? In society we have various causal mechanisms at play: government power, money, religious ideologies, and human psychology.

For years, I have felt like I have straddled two worlds; one of the intellectual Political Scientist and the other of the practical man who actually busts his ass for a living. As far has this book is concerned, I'll be pulling on my "intellectual" knowledge (for whatever that's worth), and will lay it out in simple reasonable terms like we communicate on a job site and comedians do when they are pointing out the insanity of our society. Let's pull off the panel doors of this system and see how it's wired by using common sense and the voice of reason.

"They don't want the voice of reason spoken, folks, 'cause otherwise we'd be free. Otherwise, we wouldn't believe their fucking horseshit lies, nor the fucking propaganda machine of the mainstream media and buy their horseshit products that we don't fucking need and become a third world consumer fucking plantation which is what we're becoming." -Bill Hicks

A return to Common Sense, and a renaissance of the Voice of Reason is the only thing that will insure your kids live better than you. Think good and hard at what makes a society or a country great. It always distils down to the wellbeing of the citizens and how much influence they wield in the decision making of a country. If the population are essentially debt slaves in a fundamentally broken economic system, learning in a flawed education system which

6

dumbs people down, plagued by nonstop war and terror propaganda what is going to be the result? This is the formula for centralizing power into the hands of a few, by deconstructing existing society to make them reliant upon the centers of power.

It's really not that complicated, if people ever took time to learn some history and apply some critical thought to the ideological chains that are enslaving our minds. We see the rise and fall of empires, we are marching lock step with Rome 2000 years ago. Might as well put on a toga and throw an orgy. We see the errors of the past resembling themselves in the present. History may not repeat itself, but it sure as hell rhymes. The future is becoming more bleak for the young, kids are moving back home after college unable to make their own way, incarceration rates rising, political and economic systems starting to buckle under their collective stress.

People being governed must start to wake up to Common Sense and realize how bad they have been collectively fucked over by a systems which is starting to crumble from within. Sometimes you need to step outside the structure to make an assessment before you get covered in debris. Around 2000 years ago a Roman Comedian named Juvenal was making astute observations just as many of today's comedians. He had this to say.

"Already long ago, from when we sold our vote to no man, the People have abdicated our duties; for the People who once upon a time handed out military command, high civil office, legions - everything, now restrains itself and anxiously hopes for just two things: bread and circuses." –Juvenal (circa 100 AD).

People didn't take what he was saying seriously either, the term juvenile came from his name. When Patton Oswalt said, "Knowing comedy is to know human nature" he was spot on. We have become a country of bread and circuses. For God's sake look at the popularity of Kardashians, Honey Booboo, and the fast food industry. All that seems to matter is being fed shitty food and being entertained. Meanwhile, we have all these systemic problems which are turning this country inside out and damaging the prospects of the common people.

"There is a cult of ignorance in the United States, and there always has been. The strain of anti-intellectualism has been a constant thread winding its way through our political and cultural life, nurtured by the false notion that democracy means that my ignorance is just as good as your knowledge." -Isaac Asimov.

We need to start to listen to the Voice of Reason and return to Common Sense collectively. If we don't, we are fucking over our kids. Now start thinking for ourselves! Pickup that intellectual sledge hammer God gave you (if you're an atheist nature provided), and start knocking down the bullshit. In a world of digital media, agenda pushing, and click-bate stories has developed "sound-bite" culture fueled by profits. This environment has fostered "sound-bite" thinkers. Everything has to appeal to emotion rather than to logic. This is what sells advertising and what influences the masses politically.

As a result, intellectual thought and dialog has been dwindling to a very soft murmur. What kind of effect is this having on our collective psyche? Just think about various news programs. They set up the "Brady Bunch" boxes on the television and install some talking heads to yell at each other. They're ideological wind-up dolls pushing our cognitive bias buttons for profit. They pound their ideological drums spewing logical fallacies then walk away with fat paychecks like they accomplished something. Albert

Einstein said something profound which applies today if we care to improve our situation.

"Out of clutter, find simplicity. From Discord, find Harmony. In the middle of difficulty lies opportunity." Albert Einstein

Throughout the ages there have been times in history when people have stepped forward with a message of societal warnings. They came from outside the power establishments and served as the voice of reason in an otherwise crazy world. These voices from the "wilderness" have had various names through history: prophets, philosophers, comedians, intellectuals, and etc. The one common thread that runs through these individuals is their ability to think outside of their culture with an understanding of the various forces at play. As events proceed, marching through time, more and more voices from the wilderness are chiming in at the current state of political and economic corruption. The institutional insanity we are subjected to will not be fixed from within, it's a machine built from apathy and greed where its insanity benefits a few. It's time to start moving the inertia of society in a direction that makes common sense.

Let's reason together, figure some things out, and try to laugh at the insanity.

Chapter 1

Ideology and why we think what we think...

Understanding our own mental processes gives us insight into the mind of the masses and this crazy world. If we understand the processes involved and the stimuli which guides our thoughts we can gain a greater awareness which promotes understanding and deeper level thought. Traditionally, this kind of thinking was taught in schooling going back to the Ancient Greek Civilization up until the mid-1800's. It was known as the Trivium method. A lot of today's mental health therapy seems aimed at helping people sift through thoughts in a productive manner. It begs' the question, wouldn't society be better off if we taught all young people thinking skills? This ability to freely think and measure out ideas is our most valuable asset as a human being.

"The only thing you really have is your opinion. The other things in life you're kind of borrowing... If you are going to do this thing where you go, well I'm down with this side because I'm a Hillary fan or this side because I'm Trump fan. I'm a Lakers fan or whatever fan. You've really lost your opinion. The one thing you really own... If that is the way you are rolling through life then you really have given up the one human quality that is probably the most precious. Which is being able to weigh things, examine things, and then make a declaration as to how you feel about these things. That's all you get to carry around all day if you are a human being. If your opinions are just made like, I'm a Ram's fan and a democrat. I'm

done thinking... That makes you kind of an animal. You won't evolve, change, or grow." –Adam Carolla

Thoughts must be examined, otherwise our awareness is minimal to the problems which affect us. The ideas we hold, and how those influences us day in and day out must be explored. These ideas shape our thoughts originate from our culture and surroundings. This is where ideology enters the room. The term ideology came into existence during the philosophical and political struggles of the French Revolution. There are many ways the term has been used, but the etymological roots are from the Greek origin defines it well, "science of ideas."

Ideology is nothing more than a set of ideas fit together to produce a framework. This ideological framework consists of structural members which represents individual ideas. This framework of thought provides the individual with a certain amount of security in an unsure world on both conscious and unconscious levels. Often times, when one of the structural members (ideas) is insecure people feel the whole structure is in peril, and unsettling feelings of angst roll in. Three things we need to understand about ourselves is: Cognitive ease, cognitive bias, and cognitive dissonance.

Cognitive ease is an important aspect of our psychology and plays a huge role in how we view the world. The things or ideas we are exposed to repeatedly "feel" true. When in fact they could be completely false. Cognitive ease is a measure of how hard your brain is working. Easy is when you are sitting in front of the TV. Hard would be when you are trying to figure something difficult out. Popularly accepted facts, or information that is portrayed in that light illicit cognitive ease. Facts we can all agree on: the sky is blue, grass is green, and dogs bark promote cognitive ease. These facts make us feel secure in what we think we know.

The trouble with cognitive ease is when it is artificially created for a purpose. This happens in the media all the time. A discerning mind can spot these tactics if they are aware of their existence. We have to overcome the monkey brain which evolved overtime to see threats. New patterns are met with suspicion, and the familiar patterns are met with cognitive ease. Repeating the stimulus over and over again in time; our minds will start to assume what is being said is correct, even if it is completely void of reason or truth.

Think to yourself how many times people repeat things over and over again trying to prove a point that is complete void of logic or completely false. News stories that repeatedly run are trying to evoke emotion. The 24hr news cycle is molding people perceptions. Catchy tag lines that keep repeating which have no footing in reality, "Hope and Change", "Make America Great", or "Stronger Together". These tag lines are used to shape our thinking, that is why there are so many slogans. How about a real slogan people really want to hear "Oust the Assholes". That's a real platform because it gets to the heart of the problem, corrupt assholes on both sides of the isle.

Instead, we get Phatic language to share feelings or establish a mood of sociability rather than to communicate information or ideas. Phatic language is the communication of one night stands. Just as in politics somebody is going to get fucked and will regret it later (American public). Empty speech with the express purpose of persuasion. Reading, seeing, or hearing what's familiar feels good even if it makes no sense or is completely idiotic. As humans we like what feels familiar, this is the singular reason reality TV has been able to produce "stars" out of know nothing, talentless, douchebags. These people are electronically piped into your house and become familiar, cognitive ease sets in, and these people gain a following because your brain is processing them with cognitive ease.

13

They become part of your world. The same applies to newscasters and the information they are dolling out.

An example of how this works is when uncomfortable ideas or questions are brought up which challenges our cognitive ease. We tend to shut down the idea before it's ever discussed so we can continue on in our state of cognitive ease. Hence, the idea of ignorance is bliss. For example, any valid questions to official narratives are met with "conspiracy theory" or that's "anti" or some other buzz word to shut down dialog and most people go with it because it promotes their feelings of well-being and cognitive ease. The emotion that is being felt around such exchanges should be a tip off that more exploration in thought is required, rather than slamming the door on uncomfortable ideas.

Challenging authority is always a good thing, especially when they are saying shit that doesn't make any sense. We see this with churches. A perfect example is when historical valid questions are raised which challenge the narrative of the Mormon Church. Such historically valid questions are met with that's "anti-Mormon". A lot of the time, these kinds of terms are also used to shut down dialog, and quell decent. This boils down to an attempt to call someone else crazy so we can, in many cases, keep believing in something crazy.

"The worst thing to call somebody is crazy. It's dismissive. I don't understand this person. So they're crazy. That's bullshit. These people are not crazy. They are strong people. Maybe their environment is a little sick." – Dave Chappelle

We tend to do this with all kinds of complex questions we have to answer in life. We need to realize our tendency to replace complex questions with easier irrelevant questions thereby reducing our ridiculous biases caused by cognitive ease. In turn, this feeds our confirmation bias. We need to recognize how susceptible we are to confirmation bias. We like to answer the question before we've gotten started doing research because we want to live in the world of cognitive ease. This bias leads people to ignoring relevant facts which distorts the reality of a situation. The underpinnings of confirmation bias are found in the endowment effect. Which basically means if something yours, you personally value its worth more because it's yours. This can be material items, religion, politics, etc. You think your car is work $20K when it's worth $10K. You think your kid is a great, but he's really a little asshole. Your religion is right, when all others are wrong. The list goes on and on...

"Have you ever noticed that their stuff is shit and your shit is stuff?"
–George Carlin

When incoherency within the thought system occurs contrary to reality the person holding the ideology normally undergoes cognitive dissonance. We see it all the time when people are intellectually cornered by reality or logic. They resort to anger, logical fallacies, or lying to try and hold their position. People even resort to changing the meanings of words, or all together make certain words or ideas off limits. PC culture is a direct result of cognitive dissonance. When we embrace ideas which bolster our ideologies while ignoring those that take away regardless of rationality we have programmed our brains to run off an algorithm which is contrary to reality because it feels good. If truth is important to you, you can't have it both ways.

When we take upon ourselves ideologies dealing with politics, religion, or whatever. We are in a very real sense assuming

15

the ideology's identity, and our thoughts are being molded by the endowment effect. Instead of independently drawing our conclusions on various topics we become subject to the ideology. It lords over your rational mind. Think about the words you are using. I'm a Republican. I'm a Democrat. I'm a Catholic. I'm a Vegan. I'm a Scientologist. Or whatever. The more one identifies with one of these ideological labels the more your thinking is bound to its ideals regardless of any logic or reality. Most people are born into these labels making it difficult question hard held ideas. Thinking relating to anything connected to ideology has already been done for you. Any ideas opposing an ideological topic are met automatically with emotion. Because the individual on a subconscious level is responding to what feels like a personal attack. This is the reason people get so worked up when logically weak points of their political or religious system are being examined, especially by "outsiders".

The threatening "outsiders" hails back to the days of living in tribes and small groups. We feel secure amongst our own, but outsiders seem threatening. They may take our ladies and our food. We consciously know we are not probably going to be hit over the head with a club by the "outsiders", unless you are protesting police brutality. We have biological responses and societal programming which still effects our rational judgment even if our physical safety is not being threatened. This is full on monkey brain cognition kicking in.

Our number #1 desire in life, hardwired since birth, is to feel secure in an unsecure world. It's both our strength and our folly. It's our strength when we choose to elevate our mind as individuals, and help others feel secure regardless of petty differences. Our folly when the monkey brain takes over, we push others down to feel elevated, and amplify differences which should be petty. The only way to elevate one's thinking is understand how it works. The importance of sense of security is exemplified in our language. There has been a considerable amount of study on the most powerful words in the English language. Why? Marketing of course. Attach a product to a "powerful word", people tend to be more likely to purchase it. There is some argument about the list, however the words listed are fairly accurate. There is a reason why the 12 most powerful words in the English language are: You, Discovery, Easy, Guarantee, Safety, Save, Health, Love, New, Proven, Results, and Free.

Think about it, all 12 of these words converge into one single word, security. If you want to peal a layer off security you will find peace. Feeling secure affords you with a sense of peace. This is the true unmanipulated nature of human beings. The great majority of us are inherently good, but on an unconscious level very afraid. When we get down to it we want to spend time with the people we care about, a feeling of freedom, and to be left the hell alone. We need to ask ourselves why then is the world so fucked up? When you really ponder over our modern culture, we find just about every aspect of modern life is manipulating our sense of peace and happiness for the benefit of a few which we will get into later.

We get lost in the mix of bullshit of what life should be. Unfortunately we figure it out only at the very end. When it's all but said and done, clarity of life emergences. Cultural illusions dissolve, and what we really want as individuals from life emerges. A nurse who dealt with many people over the years wrote book about the most common regrets.

1. **I wish I'd had the courage to live a life true to myself, not the life others expected of me.**
   "This was the most common regret of all. When people realize that their life is almost over and look back clearly on it, it is easy to see how many dreams have gone unfulfilled.

17

Most people had not honored even a half of their dreams and had to die knowing that it was due to choices they had made, or not made. Health brings a freedom very few realize, until they no longer have it."

2. I wish I hadn't worked so hard.

"This came from every male patient that I nursed. They missed their children's youth and their partner's companionship. Women also spoke of this regret, but as most were from an older generation, many of the female patients had not been breadwinners. All of the men I nursed deeply regretted spending so much of their lives on the treadmill of a work existence."

3. I wish I'd had the courage to express my feelings.

"Many people suppressed their feelings in order to keep peace with others. As a result, they settled for a mediocre existence and never became who they were truly capable of becoming. Many developed illnesses relating to the bitterness and resentment they carried as a result."

4. I wish I had stayed in touch with my friends.

"Often they would not truly realize the full benefits of old friends until their dying weeks and it was not always possible to track them down. Many had become so caught up in their own lives that they had let golden friendships slip by over the years. There were many deep regrets about not giving friendships the time and effort that they deserved. Everyone misses their friends when they are dying."

5. I wish that I had let myself be happier.

"This is a surprisingly common one. Many did not realize until the end that happiness is a choice. They had stayed stuck in old patterns and habits. The so-called 'comfort' of familiarity overflowed into their emotions, as well as their physical lives. Fear of change had them pretending to others, and to their selves, that they were content, when deep within, they longed to laugh properly and have silliness in their life again."

When we think about what we universally value, we need to think about the systems of government, economics, and ideologies which govern our lives which are prohibiting us from actualizing our potential and recognizing what is truly important. What we want in life is fairly simple. Therefore, how it is obtained should be somewhat simplex. The convoluted cluster fuck we are dealing with is stealing away the true purpose of life and its meaning right from under our noses. We refuse to see it until the very end of life, and that is a tragedy. The main thing keeping this going is subscribing to shitty ideas which reinforce wasted life.

In today's digital age, the ability to reinforce cognitive bias is huge, no matter how stupid the idea. It seems even if the idea is idiotic, might equals right. The problem with this is it breaks away from logic, and never ends well if human happiness is the ultimate goal. Ideology, the science of ideas, needs evaluation similar to the scientific method. The methodology of how to think is not taught in our educational system, therefore, we have a huge gap between societal progress and scientific progress. Ideological adherence without application of critical thought has created every human catastrophe with the exception of natural disasters and some diseases. Every idea within an ideology needs to be rigorously blasted by the words "how" and "why", and see where things go naturally as a result. Breaking free from ideology and questioning is scary, but needs to be done if we can find common ground to evolve as species. We can keep being apes and throwing shit at each other when we hear something we don't like, or we can have constructive dialog, find common ground, and accomplish really cool shit.

"If you attach your mind to any ideology, you're going to be on a road, and that road may or may not lead you in a good direction. But you're gonna stay on that road because you are attached to an ideology. It could be a terrible road, but you stick with it regardless of rational thinking." -Joe Rogan

Idols and Ideology

Ideology has been around since people had the ability to manipulate and be manipulated. As a kid, I was raised in a religious household, and was exposed to the various stories in the Bible. When you are young, there's not much choice whether or not you are going to Sunday School. My mind never followed the direction they were trying to make it go. I had a hard time with accepting everything literally, instead I would see if there were any symbolic messages I could accept that could offer a lesson. One Sunday I was sitting there in class probably 10 years old, not long after reading about Greek Gods in our encyclopedia set we had at home. We were being taught about Moses and the 10 Commandments.

We all know the story. The teacher explains that the Children of Israel were hanging out below the mountain when Moses climbed it to hang out with God. While he was gone the Children of Israel decided to go back to worshipping idols, specifically a golden calf. When Moses came back, he was pissed and threw the tablets down and broke them because they weren't ready for the new law. He went up the mountain for a return trip to see God and game back with the 10 Commandments.

I raised my hand and asked three questions. 1) How did you think Moses' conversation with God went when he had to go back? Probably not well was the answer. 2) Why didn't God want them worshipping idols and what do think was on that first set of tablet? Common sentiment was it was silly to worship a graven image, and God said no. However, I wanted to know what was God's reasoning. I figured if God said to do something there should be a logical reason. A 10 year old heretic, good thing I didn't live 300 years earlier in Europe. From my Encyclopedia research, I understood that idols and gods were worshipped and they all had their own rules and people would think weird beliefs associated to their idols etc.

Without realizing it at the time, I understood these idols had their own ideologies. I brought this up as a possible explanation, but it was met with, "well, we just don't know, and the lesson is we do what God says." 3) My third question, "Do you think the Golden Rule was on the first set of tablets?" My logic for the commandments was that the second set must have been more strict if they screwed up and weren't ready for the first set.

When I got in trouble as a kid, normally harsher rules were applied. In class, I wondered maybe Moses was trying to give them the Golden Rule. That idea again was met with skepticism rather than wonder. There were two lessons I learned that day from the

Bible and my Sunday school class. 1. Ideologies have been around for a long time. 2. Ideologies are still controlling how people think because of people's inability to think outside of the official narrative.

My Golden Rule: Do unto others as you would have them do unto you. If you can't do that, just don't be a dick. -Author

Breaking Ideology

The only way to break free from ideologies is understanding your relationship with reality. Questioning assumptions and applying reason is the melting down of your golden calf. Ideologies normally are packaged and pushed onto people by those who benefit from this sort of thinking. Most religious, political, and economic ideologies always has someone who grossly benefit by nature of the ideology in and of itself. Red flags and alarm bells should be going off when somebody is getting rich and powerful by you believing what they say and the benefit is far from mutual. Normally, they are full of shit.

"Loyal people go through the most bullshit while fakes get away with all kinds of bullshit." Dave Chappelle

Everything you know as reality is broadcast to your brain via your 5 senses. People run off an algorithm of pattern recognition programmed into our DNA as a survival mechanism which is formed by our experiences throughout life. Patterns emerge and we respond. If something looks like a snake we jump without thinking about it. If a situation appears threatening the fight or flight response is triggered to defend ourselves or run like hell. This biochemical response is fundamental to our survival. If it wasn't, our ancestors would have been lion food. This pattern recognition is happening on two levels; the conscious and unconscious levels of your mind. That

21

is why you'll jump when you see something out of the corner of your eye without consciously recognizing the threat. A pattern was recognized unconsciously that made you react before your conscious mind noticed. This primitive mechanism is at play in a tribal sense, are they with us or against us? I need to decide quickly, or I might get a club to the head.

This same mechanism is at play continually throughout our lives regardless if we want to admit it. What does this have to do with ideology? Ideology programs the patterns we recognize consciously and unconsciously. Day in and day out ideology is reinforced by influences that surround us. Media, friends, family, etc. all play into the programming of ideology and thinking patterns. This is why we love hearing news that confirms our own biases even if it's not factual. We see this manifest in how news is portrayed. Due to profit motive and to influence the masses, news is now modeled to reconfirming ideological biases which are subject to our basest of biological processes.

When you hear something which undermines your ideology, your security is being threaten and stress hormones are released. Stress hormones such as cortisol are not pleasant so our unconscious mind will try to avoid this feeling by directing our conscious mind to safety. During fMRI testing cognitive dissonance experience led to higher levels of activation in several brain regions. Metaphorically, more gears are turning. On the other side of the coin, when we hear something that supports our ideology and makes us feel secure, the feel good hormones such as serotonin and dopamine are released. In a real sense information we process with our brains affects us like a drug.

Don't believe me? Site two people side by side holding opposing ideologies. Share with them a piece of information which is good news for one and horrible for the other. They will experience very different emotions, and neurological responses even if this information has no real world effect on them. Think about sports fans whose week is wrecked or made with the win or loss of their team. Information we process through our sense affects us like a drug in some cases. Porn runs of this same function as well. Information being process resulting in strong neurological and biological responses.

The place in mind where information we receive by our senses intersects with our ideologies dictates the direction of our conscious minds. If somebody has been abused, a lot more situations seem threatening. A lot more patterns of potential trauma exist in the mind. The old adage is true "when you are holding a hammer everything looks like a nail". The only way to get ahold of the unconscious mind is consciously being mindful. This is the reason counseling works, and this is the reason AA works. People feel safe exploring the sensitive thought patterns which regulate their emotions in a supportive environment, and find their true sense of self. This is process of making YOUR mind YOUR bitch, rather than being emotionally controlled by it, which leaves you open to be manipulated by others and unknowingly by yourself.

"There is no society in human history that ever suffered because its people became too reasonable." -Sam Harris

When somebody's opinion changes on an ideology there is a tendency to throw the baby out with the bath water. The good ideas which were part of the ideology are cast by the wayside, and a whole new set of ideas are accepted as a way of doing things. The problem with this sort of thinking is that's analogous with running from buzz saw but into the wood chipper. In other words, trading in bullshit for horseshit, or horseshit for bullshit. Most of the time you're dealing with shit unless done mindfully deconstruct the formation of the idea or opinion. Ideas or principles are a lot like finding a diamond in a patch of gravel. When you notice the glistening reflection in the sun, you stop, pick it up and examine it. Do you just put in your pocket without first closely examining it? Probably not, you'd have pockets full of rocks and your pants would fall down. You'll look at is closely from various angles to judge whether it is worth putting it into your pocket. We question ourselves if we deemed it beautiful, if so you hold onto it. Otherwise, you leave it in the dirt. This should be the same practice we use when thinking about thoughts or ideals we hold. The good news is, when you can recognize what's shit, its great fertilizer for new ideas to sprout up and grow. If we are not mindful, these thought processes leads us into the mother of mental paradoxes the Dunning Kruger Effect.

Too Stupid to Know you're Stupid

Yes, it's a real thing. All of the discussed thought processes are unfortunately housed under the umbrella of the Dunning – Kruger effect. It is a cognitive bias in which low-ability individuals suffer from illusory superiority. People will think they are smarter than they really are, sing better than they really do, or funnier than they really are. Arguably this is a trait that afflicts those with narcissistic personalities and those with very rigid thinking patterns.

The phenomenon of Dunning – Kruger effect has been around for millennia, but these are the first two academics to formally test and study it. David Dunning and Justin Kruger from the department of psychology at Cornell University found, "Across four studies, the authors found that participants scoring in the bottom quartile on tests of humor, grammar, and logic grossly overestimated their test performance and ability. Although test scores put them in the 12th percentile, they estimated themselves to be in the 62nd." We

24

can now understand why there are so many "epic fail" videos on the internet. Plus, this stupidity is celebrated to an extent by the recognition for fame it can garner. Depending on the way you want to take Forest Gump's momma's words, it fits this situation well.

"Stupid is as stupid does." –Forrest Gump's Mamma

This personal disconnect with reality stems from one key psychological problem. I lack of self-awareness. This is a death blow to the real capacity of human consciousness. The ancient Greeks understood the importance of self-awareness as inscribed "gnothi seauton" in the forecourt of the Temple of Apollo, which means "know thyself." This lack of self-awareness has been propagated by our media, education system, and rigid ideologies. It's also promoted in the trend of helicopter parenting where kids are told they are good at everything.

Instead of viewing reality as one great mosaic which portrays an image coherent with objective reality. People are only looking at pieces they choose to look at, arraign them as they see fit, and pretend that's all there is. This is where the intellectual slaying line of "my feelings are good as your feelings" comes from. This shuts down any dialog of any real value and quickly devolves into grown adults debating topics like upset toddlers. Self-awareness is a lot like being able to see in color vs. seeing only in black and white. If you are not aware of self, how can you be aware of the rest of the world? Could there be facts and nuances that we are missing or refuse to see? If this is not the case, why do we have so many highly educated dumb asses? Noble Loiret and great thinker Bertrand Russell noted, "One of the painful things about our time is that those who feel certainty are stupid, and those with any imagination and understanding are filled with doubt and indecision."

Painful indeed, how does this play out in society as a whole? I'll give you a hint, look at any Republican or Democratic political rally. I find it fascinating that the best analysis on certain topics don't come from the media, but from people who claim they don't know anything. A lot of these people are comedians, and a comedic mind unbound by ideology is much more powerful than society gives credit. It's interesting how someone can start off by saying "I don't know anything" or "I don't know shit", and come to societal conclusions which are correct or profound. Why is that? It's because logic is being used in the formation of ideas.

"Real knowledge is to know the extent of one's ignorance" - *Confucius*

4 Categories of Knowing

Intellectual honesty and emotional maturity is required. An important part of knowing something is being able to weigh information. What's source of information? What are the inherent weakness to the idea? Does what is being said or claimed make sense? Any money behind what is being claimed? Motivation behind information is an extremely important factor which should always be identified.

1. You know what you know. This is something you have personally experienced via your senses. The cause and effect relationship of ideas are coherent, and you understand the outcome of certain criteria. No matter how the idea is scrutinized the truth is self-evident, the proof can be experienced by your senses. If you find yourself thinking you know something, explore the idea from another angle and see how it holds up.

2. You know what you think you know. People have a hard time with this one. This is probability thinking, but people love absolutes in a world drenched with fear and filled to the brim in horseshit. This is the ability to suspend emotion on a subject, scrutinize it, and identify information holes in the coherency of ideas. This is being prudent, or the application of common sense. Being wrong or changing one's mind because more information came to   light is perfectly acceptable. We see politicians flip flop on various topics, normally it's for political gain. Wouldn't it make sense if they explained their reasoning to see if any of it made sense? A prudent population armed with common sense would demand transparency of those that govern over them.

3. You know what you don't know. On some subjects this is easy to admit. I do not know rocket science. It gets tricky when assumptions are made which are promoted as fact if it fits within the parameters of an ideology or someone's thinking. We end up saying we know something just because it makes us feel good or secure. Instead of constructive discourse emotion gets in the way, because if the ideology attached to one's sense of self. This is where sucking it up, and saying I was wrong comes into play. However, identifying what you don't know is the place in the mind where a thirst for knowledge is acquired.

4. You don't know what you don't know. Curiosity and a sense of wonder has been at the heart of every human innovation. This sense of wonder is at the heart of Renaissance and every other era of human enlightenment. What else is out there? What ideas can change mankind for the better? What is the true nature of reality? When you wonder about what you don't know, ideas tend to take form. The words "I don't

know, but I'm going to find out", or "I'm going to find a way" really take on meaning.

The problem with any ideology is that it gives answers before you evaluate the problem. Rather than espousing ideological banter as a cure to problems; work to understand the problem then rendering actual solutions is what works in reality regardless of ideology. Who cares who laid claim to the idea as long as the solution works? It's time to forget ideologies that work against us.

"The ideas of true debate, honest discussion, and fact based reason are crossing the political divide in a way nothing else is doing right now. It may not translate into this election the way we want it to, and it may not stop regressive attitudes from corrupting your minds tomorrow, but have no doubt, the game is on." -Dave Rubin

Interesting Information:

Ware, Bonnie. *The Top Five Regrets of The Dying. Hay House.* 2012.

Kruger, Justin; Dunning, David (1999). "Unskilled and Unaware of It: How Difficulties in Recognizing One's Own Incompetence Lead to Inflated Self-Assessments"

Chapter 2

Origins of Comedy and its role in Society.

The Ancient Greeks

The historical role of comedy in society is often over looked, but important factor when identifying social problems. Plus, laughing makes people happy. It's been said laughter is the sound of the soul dancing. Life is a struggle of finding happiness and battling misery. In this case the only prudent way to achieve the context of comedy in society is a brief history lesson. When we dig back far enough, we find what we characterize as comedy is from ancient Greece. It's quite interesting how much the Ancient Greek civilization gave us.

Pretty much every large system of thought which supports the bedrock of Western Civilization came from the Ancient Greeks. Most of what we get to enjoy in Western Civilization was seeded in minds of Ancient Greeks. Some believe this learning came to the Greeks from Egypt. These people were smart as fuck for their time. Very interesting how the application of logic, reason, and common sense came up with the ideas which made our civilization great. How does Greece get repaid for its priceless contributions 2000 years later you may ask? With crushing debt and a refugee crisis of epic proportions of course. Thanks for your great ideas now go fuck off. The question we all should be asking is, why they were so damn smart and how did they get that way? Here's a short list of things they contributed:

1. Democratic Government - A pretty good idea if you want peace. History has shown that being ruled by a dictator or a group of ruling elite doesn't work out well for the common folk.
2. The Olympics – It's a fun spectacle of sport that brings the world together unless you're on the naught list.

3. The Hippocratic Oath - An oath to take care of people needing medical help. Too bad there isn't a part of the oath about the financial hemorrhaging that is occurring while your brain hemorrhage is being treated.

4. Architectural Design - They definitely made some cool shit. In fact, if you look at a lot of our government building you can see where we used their designs.

5. Math - They had a group of math Geeks name after Pythagoras who applied deduction and reason to mathematical theorem. This guys measured the shit out of everything and figured out there is some reason behind the madness of nature.

6. Philosophical Reasoning - The big names in philosophical thought came from Greece. Socrates, Plato, and Aristotle to name a few. What they gave us was the application of evidence based reasoning to explain life. They would deductively reason why things are the way they are, rather than just saying the Gods made it that way.

7. The Marathon - Not sure how big of a contribution this is, but the story behind the Marathon is bad ass. In around 500 B.C. the Persian arm invaded Greece. Quick side note, Western Civilization even in its infancy has been warring with people from that area of the world. Nothing new, remember history rhymes. The Greek army was outnumbered and sent a local runner Pheidippides to get help and warn people. He's basically like Paul Rever, but without the horse, poor bastard. He ran 280 miles in under 10 days then died at the end. Literally, ran himself to death. If he is sitting in heaven somewhere looking down he must think people who run half marathons are complete pussies.

8. The Theater - In ancient Greece functioned in a way the internet does today when it comes to expressing ideas. Unlike today, it wasn't owned by large corporate interest, but was open to people from all walks of life. There were dramas, tragedies, and comedies which served to communicate social and political concerns.

9. Comedy - It is likely there was comedy before ancient Greece, but this is probably the best documentation of it early beginnings. There were people like Aristophanes who would mix political, social, and literary satire. Not much unlike a John Oliver who points out the ridiculousness of some of our societal neurosis and broken government systems. Others like Menander wrote plays ridiculing the upper elites of the day. "Punching up" has been around for a long time. It's fundamental to a free and open society.

Part of the reason why comedy sprang up in Greece so predominately was due to its underpinnings of philosophical thought. They both utilize the Socratic function of questioning ourselves and society. These early comedians had applied logic and were very aware of societal norms and the cultural fabric. One such early philosopher if living today would be a standup comedian, Diogenes of Sinope. In fact Alexander the Great once said, "If I were not Alexander, I should wish to be Diogenes." He fucked with Plato all the time by showing up to Plato's school and goading him. He also is likely the first person in recorded history who made a dick joke when he mused about beating off. Once he saw the officials of a temple hauling someone off who had stolen a bowl belonging to the treasury, and commented.

"The great thieves are leading away the little thief". -Diogenes of Sinope

In some respects not much has changed in two thousand years if you consider some of the comments made by contemporary comedians. Illustrating the fact that for some strange reason, the people running religions always want your money. Somehow this message from God only falls on the religious leaders' ears, good thing they rely the message to the rest of us...

"God's everywhere but we gotta go down there to see him? Really?! And he's mad at me down there and I owe you money?... It's stupid. It's ridiculous." -Bill Burr

The Dark Ages

This was bad time for the cynic or comedian, it would likely lead to death if you got too mouthy. Hundreds of years of dogmatic oppression of contrasting viewpoints. Once thought, and intellectual dialog was once held in high regard lead way to the crushing reactionary oppression of those in power. Namely by the church and those considered royalty. The powers that be had a monopoly on thought.

This is the Political Correctness of the Middle Ages, make no mistake. Both are forms of silencing of words, ideas, and thoughts. Literacy was low, the collective psyche was largely sculpted by the Church of Rome. A smart ass in those days would have been considered a dangerous individual. Why? He would have made people think outside of the lines of the societal structure controlled by the ruling elite. Since the beginning of time people in control

33

have always known the power they have is built upon the thinking of those below them.

Elaborate ideas have been created to propagate such myths which people have bought into for generations. The Devine Right of Kings is such an example. In and of itself is a logical fallacy called "The Appeal to Heaven". This fallacy basically states, God says it's this way so don't question. A lot of real estate within in that logical fallacy to come up with a lot of bullshit. In fact, this insanity went so far as to appoint someone to the position of the "Groom of the Stool." Yes, it is as it sounds. There were noble people who were royal ass wipers to the king, this position was finally discontinued in 1901 in England. WTF, should have been on everyone's lips when these ideas were being forced on them. Within this lovely time in history thinking was rigorously controlled, and fear is tool to corral thought.

"There once was a time when all people believed in God and the church ruled. This time was called the Dark Ages." -Richard Lederer

There were only a few places that comedy was permitted, but on the whole free thinking a vital component of comedy was silenced. First, was at the court where jesters were allowed to do some social commentary. Their job was primarily to entertain the King and his Court. Obviously in such a position being too critical could lead to unwanted consequences. However, that was risky business depending on the whims of the King and the Church. The second form of comedy to a less extent was permitted is some festival plays.

"In the middle ages of Christianity opposition to the State was hushed. The consequence was, Christianity became loaded with all the Romish follies. Nothing but free argument, raillery and even ridicule will preserve the purity of religion." -Thomas Jefferson

As you can see the Dark Ages was a huge step backwards in constructive dialog. For the Greeks very little was off limits for ridicule and joking. The Dark Ages dealt a blow to cynical comedy, the application of logic and reason, and dick jokes. It took hundreds of years to get back dick jokes!

The Renaissance

This was an era of enlightenment, and a liberation of minds and boobs. Within intellectual circles this had to be one of the most exciting times to be alive. Old ideas rediscovered from classical Greek, and new ideas being created. All the while, there was a resurgence in cleavage! The underappreciated act of "Motorboating" returned without anyone knowing what a motorboat actually is. In addition to an explosion of bust-lines there was also an explosion of critical thought and vast innovations in: art, science, architecture, technology, philosophy, and even comedy. Renaissance literally means, "Rebirth" in French. The human mind figuratively left its dark recesses of confinement and stepped into the light of day. Seeking wisdom and innovation was valued in society over dogma. There was excitement surrounding new ideas and progress. Of course, when new ideas and modalities of thought emerge which emboldens the individual the power structures in control tend to react. We can see this in how the Catholic Church reacted when they lost their monopoly on religious thought. The use of military force and the Roman Inquisition were utilized to attempt to put the cat back in the bag. Isn't interesting how power structures all act the same when challenged? Ad Hominem Argument, circular reasoning, and host of other logical fallies are going to be grind up, put in a cannon and shot your way. Some real Wizard of Oz shit, "Pay no attention to the man behind the curtain". They all want the critical parties silenced. Think of the fates of Edward Snowden and other whistleblowers...

"Nothing strengthens authority so much as silence." Leonardo da Vinci

During this period of time a new kind of comedy emerged with the blending in of classical Latin Comedy which led to Elizabethan Comedy. Notables of this comedic expression where the likes of William Shakespeare and Ben Johnson. This man Shakespeare, who had the ability to be a comedic writer has had the biggest influence on the language we speak second only to the Bible.

This evolution of comedic thought led to thinkers like Oscar Wilde. Wilde, for Victorian England would have been considered a wild man. He came from a well to-do family that was somewhat dysfunctional family. Makes me wonder if sometimes dysfunction can leads to a perception of life that promotes comedic thinking and deeper thinking? The more difficult something is, the harder one normally thinks. He was educated at a good university and was a free-thinker. He produced comedic works that enraged critics and some of society because he questioned and ridiculed certain components of morality in Victorian England. He was bisexual which caused him to be imprisoned. However, one has to wonder how much of his work played into his prosecution of being in a homosexual relationship. If you piss off those in power, look out for trumped up charges such as in Jullian Assage's case.

Too bad Wilde was not alive today. If we was, he and Milo Yainnopoulos would probably form the greatest Gay Power Couple in history. Armed with their fabulous hair and tenacious intellect they would destroy their advisories with their witty gay logic. Here's the thing about the gay issue I do not understand. As a straight guy, shouldn't you be relieved? There is a number of highly manicured and witty guys leaving the pussy pool to go bob for dicks. Shouldn't that be greatest news ever? If it was a strategic decision you'd buy your gay buddy a beer and thank him for creating a demand in the market for your dirty ass. You can't compete with these dudes, they have been their Mom's best friend for years. They're fucking sensitive. They understand the woman enigma while we like how it looks.

If you want to tell people the truth, make them laugh, otherwise they'll kill you. -Oscar Wilde

Comedy of the Modern Era

There have been many book and articles written on the development of comedy in this era. Therefore, I'm not going to go down the pathway of development from slapstick, to verbal humor, to surreal comedy, and the development of modern day stand-up comedy.

For the purpose of this book, I want to spotlight some of the intellectual comedians who challenged our perceptions of reality and make people think as we discuss various issues plaguing our society. Many of these people have been under appreciated luminaries in our world. People quoted or mentioned are by no means an exhaustive list, but is here merely to serve as a means to illustrate many comedians have the ability share insights of truth with others. Like prophets of old, their vision and insights provide truth to the human condition. In many cases, these truth tellers' messages resonate beyond their lifetimes because of the power of their words. When we think of these people's lives we see a pattern emerge in how they were treated because of the words they were sharing. They put to voice what we are all thinking on a conscious or unconscious level counter to what society wants us to believe or say. The truth cuts its own path. Below are 4 examples of people who brought truth to the surface via their comedy during their lifetimes.

"All truths Passes through three stages. First, it is ridiculed, second it is violently opposed, and third, it is accepted as self-evident." Arthur Schopenhauer - Philospher.

Lenny Bruce

He brilliantly pushed his audiences in a Socratic, self-questioning style that ranged widely over the social landscape, unearthing taboos and exposing them for their absurdities and contradictions. Bruce said, "Sometimes I look at life in the fun mirror at a carnival. I see myself as a profound, incisive wit, concerned with man's humanity to man. Then I stroll to the next mirror and I see a pompous, subjective ass whose humor is hardly spiritual. I see traces of Mephistopheles. All my humor is based on destruction and despair." His irreverence toward authority was epic. On so many levels he pointed out the emperor had no clothes. Bruce was constantly hounded by law-enforcement officials who frequented his shows and arrested him.

Richard Pryor

He spoke with complete frankness about racism, sex and pain: subjects on which, as a black American who had a rough childhood was well qualified to speak. It also meant using his own voice, the jive-talk of black urban America, liberally using the words "nigger" and "motherfucker". He gave a strong voice to the underprivileged black community by being a fearless observer of society and pointing out the folly and failures of widely held beliefs.

George Carlin

He went deep, he didn't want to deal with topical humor. He took the sledge hammer of intellect and readily used it in his analysis of our culture. He went down the rabbit holes of abortion, religion, patriotism, rape, mass murder, God, suicide, random disasters and of course, that sport of fat white business cocksuckers - Golf. His brilliance was exemplified in his analysis of bastardization of the English language, and how it's been manipulated to influence the masses by politicians.

Joan Rivers

She became a comedian in the world of comedy when it was almost exclusively male. Nothing was off limits, and that's what made her a force in the comedy world which opened doors for other women. She had the ability to not take herself too seriously while broaching serious or sensitive subjects. While playing a small venue in Wisconsin, and a man with a deaf son took offense to a Helen Keller joke. "Let me tell you what comedy is about," Rivers fires back. "Comedy is to make everybody laugh at everything and deal with things," also mentioning, "I had a deaf mother."

Bill Hicks

Fellow iconoclast Tom Waits described Hicks as a "blowtorch, excavator, truthsayer, and brain specialist. He will correct your vision. Others will drive on the road he built." Bill Hicks' comedic achievement is somewhat miraculous, when you put his comedy into the context of the time he did it. This was the 1980's and very early 90's. He spotlighted the realities of society people are now only starting to wake up to now, in large part due to the internet. He spoke about everything from the news cycles, mounting anti-intellectualism, and government corruption.

Chapter 3

Education

"Stupid people can be educated; crazy people can be medicated, but there is only one cure for ignorant people who choose to stay that way - suffering." – Over two thousand years of history.

Education plays a foundational role in the life of an individual and society. It molds our perceptions, it gives us tools and useful knowledge we can draw upon to create a successful life. One of the ways our society stratifies itself is along the lines of education. The more education someone receives the more respected they are in their field, and by others in general. The message has been the more you learn the more you earn. The reality of this message seems to be breaking down. The mounting student loan debt, and high level of college educated under employed millennials should be an indicator that something isn't right.

"Essentially, student debt is like HPV. If you go to college, you're almost certainly going to get it. And if you so, it will follow you for the rest of your life." -John Oliver

Politicians keep banging the drum of more education. They don't give a shit about your kids' education, it makes them sound better so you'll vote for them. Appealing to people's desire to help children is always popular politically. Most of them are sending their kids to private schools. We need to spend more money on education is the common cry of the politician even though almost twice as much is spent on our schools than in other comparable countries. They come up with catchy programs "Common Core", or no "Child Left Behind".

These are nothing more than buzz words, and justification to create more bureaucracy, and funnel more money into private companies which lobby heavily to profit off this mess. According to just about every published study the academic aptitude of the US is low. I've seen ranges from 14th down to 27th spot. Either way that sucks, and throwing money at the problems seems not be working. Saying more education when the problem is likely qualitative rather than quantitative is not well thought out, problematic, and doesn't offer any sort of a remedy. How does putting more energy into any system that is qualitatively flawed going to produce better results? The results will be more of the same.

"Not too bright, folks. Not too fucking bright. But if you talk to one of them about this, if you isolate one of them, you sit 'em down rationally, you talk to 'em about the low IQ's and the dumb behavior and the bad decisions; right away they start talking about education. That's the big answer to everything: Education. They say, 'We need more money for education. We need more books, more teachers, more classrooms, more schools. We need more testing for the kids!' You say to 'em, 'Well, you know, we've tried all that and the kids still can't pass the tests'. They say, 'Aw, don't you worry about that, we're gonna lower the passing grades!' And that's what they do in a lot of these schools now, they lower the passing grades so more kids can pass. More kids pass, the school looks good, everybody's happy; the IQ of the country slips another two or three points and pretty soon, all you'll need to get into college is a fucking pencil! 'Gotta pencil? Get the fuck in there, it's physics!' Then everyone wonders why 17 other countries graduate more scientists than we do. Education!" - George Carlin

Prussian Education System

At this juncture, wouldn't it be prudent to get some background on this fucked up system everyone is complaining about? Notice how nobody really ever talks about the history of this system, and the influences behind its creation. With any broken system, you need to know its history to gain context and understanding. You don't go the doctor with liver failure, and leave

43

out your history of hitting the bottle every day for years do you? I guess only if you want to deny the reality of history. So let's head to Prussia in the 1800's to get some answers.

The first person we need to identify in the creation of this system was named Horace Mann. He is credited with the creation of America's public education system. He was a member of the US House of Representatives and served as an educator. In 1837, he became the head of the newly created Board of Education in Massachusetts where the establishment of the first public education system took place. At the time he was looking at various educational styles in the world and ran across the system used in Prussia which today is Germany. The Prussian government was very happy about their educational system because it had done so well fulfilling the government's purposes.

Mann and a few of his fellow educators traveled to Prussia to study their system. Upon return to the US they lobbied heavily to institute the Prussian system. For the next 30 years US dignitaries came to Germany and earned degrees. After returning home they started to staff all the major universities in the country. When Horace Mann became the Secretary of Education he promoted his new concept.

"The state is the father of children." -Horace Mann

It was the state's responsibility to ensure education was provided by the state for the child. A good idea, making sure children are educated, but how is education going to be defined? It's a very broad subject spanning all areas of thought and the accumulation of all human knowledge. After Massachusetts accepted the Prussian education system, it quickly spread throughout the whole country. Soon after the end of the Civil War, Horace

Mann's sister Elizabeth Peabody, of the Peabody foundation, pushed the establishment of the Prussian system in the conquered South. By 1900 every American child grew up learning within the Prussian system.

"It is a miracle that curiosity survives formal education." -Albert Einstein

Why the Prussian system you may be asking yourself? We already had the classical education system which produced most of the great thinkers for a couple thousand years. In the 18th century, the Kingdom of Prussia was one of the first countries to introduce free and compulsory schooling. In 1806, after the Prussians were defeated by Napoleon they came to the conclusion the reason they lost the war was because Prussian solders were thinking for themselves and not following orders. Thinkers as we all know make horrible order followers. To make sure this didn't happen again a new system of education was created.

To be fair to the Prussians, it wasn't all about brainwashing, it also gave skills to the masses needed for early industrialization. Reading, writing, and arithmetic were all offered up, but in a strict format. This format taught duty, discipline, respect for authority, and the importance of following orders. The elites then went on to higher secondary education while the rest stayed in the working class. It was through this system they tried to create social obedience through indoctrination. Part of this indoctrination was being convinced that the King was just and the need for obedience was paramount. In truth the purpose of the system was to instill loyalty to the Crown and have a pool of young men ready for military service and work within the state bureaucracy. To accomplish this it was necessary to kill any independent thinking. Prussian philosopher Johann Gottlieb

Fichte was the brains behind this new system of education. He's used John Locke's view, which most of us agree, that children's minds are a blank slate. Then introduced Jean-Jacques Rousseau's ideas on how we could write on that slate. Governing factors of the Prussian education system dictated what was going to be learned, what was going to be thought about, and how long to think about it.

"My kids used to love math. Now it makes them cry. Thanks standardized testing and common core." -Louis C.K.

In order to have a policy making a ruling class and a sub class it was believed that you had to remove people's ability to make sense out of available information. In short, remove the ability to critically think. You may be thinking to yourself, WTF? This system wasn't set up for the good of the individual, but was developed for the good of the state and the ruling class. Interesting really how the average person is unaware of this history. Do you honestly think you'll get taught the history of the system designed to make you dumb, while actively making you dumb, from the dumbing down system itself? Of course not. Most teachers don't know the history. That's like a con man explaining his con while conning you while completely unaware that they are a con man. That's an analogy to make a point. I'm not calling teachers con men. For the most part they are wonderful people, and have been abused by the same system.

Research the Prussian education system apply, some Common Sense, and you'll come to the same conclusions. Read some work by John Taylor Gatto or Charlotte Iserbyt, both incredible educators and scholars. When this information settles in, you have a choice. Get pissed because there is a fair chance you and your kids could have been way smarter, or keep being stupid. Johann

Fichte, the mastermind behind this system, had the following to say about schooling. Being pissed for the right reasons is never wrong. Just make sure your reasons are just.

"The schools must fashion the person, and fashion him in such a way, that he simply cannot will otherwise than what you wish him to will." -Johann Fichte

In 1807 when Napoleon occupied Berlin, Ficthe gave a series of speeches about the supremacy of the German people above all others. His words served as a catalyst to German nationalism and the Prussian education system. He also called out the Jews, saying that they were a state with in a state which would undermine the country. He openly spoke about needing to run the Jews out of Germany. His ideas had a very large influence on the rise of the Nazism. He also has been deemed the spiritual father of neo-Nazism. Wait! What? Yes, sometimes the truth is stranger than fiction. We may want to rethink the system offering up information into the minds of the young.

"Education should aim at destroying free will so that after pupils are thus schooled they will be incapable throughout the rest of their lives of thinking or acting otherwise than as their school masters would have wished. When the techniques has been perfected, every government that has been in charge of education for more than one generation will be able to control its subjects securely without the need of armies or policemen." Johann Fichte

Into this educational nightmare walks Wilhlm Maximiliam Wundt. In 1847, at the University of Leipzig he established the world's first psychological laboratory. Wundt held the belief that man is devoid of spirit and self-determination. Originally, education meant drawing out a person's innate talents and abilities by imparting the knowledge of languages, science, history, literature, and critical thinking etc. It was Wundt's belief that:

"Learning is the result of modifiability in the path of neural conduction... This situation-response formula is adequate to cover learning of any sort, and the really influential factors in learning are readiness of the neurons, sequence in time, belongingness, and satisfying consequences" -The Leipzig Connection, Paolo Lionni.

During this time at Leipzig, study of the socialization of children rather than the development of intellect were emerging. The Prussian education system was divided into three groups. The elite which accounted for .5% who received the best education which produces people with the ability to think intellectually. About 5.5% received relschulen, and were somewhat taught how to think. The rest of the 94% went to school for dummies called volkschulen where they were taught harmony, obedience, following orders, and freedom from stressful thinking. In other words, schooling to be taught how to be stupid, submissive, and smart enough to do your job.

An important part of the system was to break the link between reading and thinking of the young child. If a child becomes too knowledgeable and capable of thinking independently they are going to start asking a lot of questions. Nothing is more terrifying to the ruling class than people who think. In the volkschulen (school for dummies), the method of teaching was to divide whole ideas into smaller subjects which did not exist prior to that time. The subjects were further broken down into periods of time during the day. With appropriate variation, no one would really know what was going on.

In a sense, it compartmentalized people's minds to the extent they don't trust their own judgment. You see this when people can't follow conversations. A perfect example of this can be heard on the *Adam and Drew Show*, when Dr. Drew struggles to keep up with Adam's logic in the formulation of ideas. It also destroys the ability to see reality and how everything has natural flow of cause and effect. Instead everything looks chaotic with no real understanding, and always reliant upon experts or authority.

Most of the compulsory schooling laws were passed by the year 1900, and all of the PhD's in America were trained in Prussia who were now in charge of this new educational system. This new government project destroyed the community one room schoolhouse. Community ties to the schooling of their own children was replaced by educational boards dictating policy.

One of the reason's the self-appointed elites brought back the Prussian system was to create a non-thinking class of workers to staff the growing industrial revolution. In 1776, 85% of people were reasonably educated and had independent livelihoods. By 1840 the percentage was still high around 70%. The ability to learn and go out on your own had to be broken so factory labor would be available. The more dependent the people, the more labor would be available for working in factories owned by the elite. This is one of major reasons why the elite of the day paid for the establishment of this style of schooling. The other reason, keep people dumb so they don't understand how bad they are getting screwed. It's fascinating to look at the educational books which were used prior to the Prussian system, and how see extremely literate people were.

This new model of schooling was quickly picked up and underwritten by the elite families of the US via their philanthropic organizations. The Rockefellers, Carnegies, Whitney, Peabody, and Ford families all took part in spreading this form of education throughout the country. In 1902, John D. Rockefeller created the General Education Board.

At the cost of $129 million, the General Education Board provided major funding for schools across the nation and was very influential in shaping the current school system. A year later in 1905, Carnegie Foundation for the Advancement of Teaching was founded and worked in step with the Rockefeller General Education Board. In 1913, Frederick T. Gates, Director of Charity for the Rockefeller Foundation, wrote the following in The Country School of Tomorrow, Occasional Papers Number 1.

"In our dream we have limitless resources, and the people yield themselves with perfect docility to our molding hand. The present educational conventions fade from our minds; and, unhampered by tradition, we work our own good will upon a grateful and responsive rural folk. We shall not try to make these people or any of their children into philosophers or men of learning or of science. We are not to raise up among them authors, orators, poets, or men of letters. We shall not search for embryo great artists, painters, musicians. Nor will we cherish even the humbler ambition to raise up from among them lawyers, doctors, preachers, statesmen, of whom we now have ample supply." -Fredrick T. Gates

This philanthropic involvement in education was nothing more than an attempt to mold society and minds of the people of this country. Add to the equation vast wealth, control of monetary policy, a large portion of the press, and politicians pretty much all areas of life where controls by a very small elite. In 1914, the National Education Association (NEA) Alarmed by the Activity of the Carnegie and Rockefeller Foundations. At an annual meeting in St.

Paul Minnesota, a resolution was passed by the Normal School Section of the NEA. An excerpt stated:

"We view with alarm the activity of the Carnegie and Rockefeller Foundations—agencies not in any way responsible to the people—in their efforts to control the policies of our State educational institutions, to fashion after their conception and to standardize our courses of study, and to surround the institutions with conditions which menace true academic freedom and defeat the primary purpose of democracy as heretofore preserved inviolate in our common schools, normal schools, and universities."

The starting point of most of this education is traced back to the University of Chicago and financing directly from the Rockefeller family. How long as a nation of people can we coast off the genius of people who lived a couple hundred years ago? Now we have the elite's calling all the shots, and an uninformed public. We have reached peak stupid. Grown-ass-adults dying from falling off cliffs, running into traffic, or being shot dead from breaking into someone's house while playing Pokemon Go. Prussian education system worked great!

Most people do not know we have been using the educational system developed by the same dude who's considered the grand-pappy of Nazism. Historians reflect that one of the biggest reasons of the rise of the Third Reich was the fact that the German people had been bread from birth to respect authority above all else and accept it without question. Just like here in America, this is called Blind Patriotism. If all over America has been raised in a system adopted by pre-Nazi Germany to dismantle critical thought how's this going to go play out for us? The indicators of where we are heading are being manifest politically, socially, and economically. Now, people who champion the Constitution are now being called radicals. When in fact, our government has gone so far from the Constitution is the root of most of our problems. One of the best lines from Norm MacDonald was on David Lettermen when he was talking about Hitler. "You know, with Hitler the more I learn about that guy the more I don't care for him. There's nothing redeeming about the guy. How on earth on earth did these Germans like follow this lunatic you know and they're like oh he was an incredible public speaker you know? He could hypnotize you with his public speaking and then I see him and he's like (screaming in harsh German tones) and I'm like what? That's not my idea of a silver tongued devil." In truth they had been molded by their educational system to accept Hitler without too many people questioning or opposing. Even Hitler knew this when he stated, "What good fortune for governments that the people do not think."

"I was on this German talk show and this woman said to me: "Mr. Williams, why do you think there is not so much comedy in Germany?" and I said: "Did you ever think you killed all the funny people?" -Robin Williams

Noam Chomsky one of the predominate scholars and minds alive today described education as follows.

"The whole educational and professional training system is a very elaborate filter, which just weeds out people who are too independent, and who think for themselves, and who don't know how to be submissive, and so on -- because they're dysfunctional to the institutions."

The effect of this educational system creates a scarcity of people able to critically think, and produces educated dumbasses. Now, the elites in our society do not subject their children to this brain damaging system. They get sent to private schools which emulate the classical education system of learning which we will get into later. We get the Common Core, or more accurately the "Commoners Core". The education for the common folk, or the peasants' education. It is the new model of the volkshulen (folks school) from 150 years ago. This education system is like a Volkswagen Bug, you replace the wheels, change the upholstery, and give it some add-ons and say wonderful things about it. It's still a bug, and will never be a Porsche.

Obviously the system isn't working. Education policy written and enforced by people who haven't spent any real time in the classroom working with children doesn't make any sense. This top down directed methodology doesn't work for a simple reason, dictatorships make people miserable. Regardless of what you want to believe this is an example of living in a society that is veering to tyranny. When power is taken from the hands of the parents, teachers, and students and given to the state without any real input from those doing the teaching is dictating. Dictate is the root word for dictatorship. This education strangle hold funnels billions of tax dollars to publishers such as Pearson and McGraw Hill who's board of directors are entangled in the highest levels of government and elite think tanks which govern US policy. The lobbying that takes place is immense. Due to this standardized teaching hell, there is an issue with what "experts" call "non-cognitive skills."

Policy makers and educators are scrambling to figure out what to do. These skills consist of persistence, self-discipline, focus, confidence, teamwork, organization, seeking help, staying on task and so on. What needs to be recognized is that the lack of these qualities are inherent in, and deliberately engineered into the Prussian education system from its inception. Whoever coined this phrase "non-cognitive skills" should be hit in their cognition free brain. Cognition comes from the Latin word "cogn", which means learn or know. Today cognition means the mental action or process of acquiring knowledge and understanding through thought, experience, or senses.

What's being described as "non-cognitive skills" are the basic traits of being a thinking human being. There is nothing "non-cognitive" about it, it's all cognition. Your heart beating, digesting food, or your hair growing is non-cognitive. Maybe they could get somewhere in fixing the problem if they called the problem what it is, human thinking skills. Non-cognition is the cause of the fucking problem in the first place! While were are at it lets call something else it is not, cancer from here on out will be known as non-cancer. Let's go full retard and change all word meanings we don't like to different words because it makes us feel better, and maybe the problems will magically disappear...

*"But I'll tell you what they don't want. They don't want a population of citizens capable of critical thinking. They don't want well-informed, well-educated people capable of critical thinking. They're not interested in that! That doesn't help them. That's against their interests. That's right! You know something? They don't want people who are smart enough to sit around the kitchen table and figure out how badly they're getting fucked by a system that threw them overboard 30 fucking years ago. They don't want that! You know what they want? They want **Obedient Workers - Obedient Workers.** People who are just smart enough to run the machines and do the paperwork but just dumb enough to passively accept all these*

increasingly shittier jobs with the lower pay, the longer hours, the reduced benefits, the end of overtime and the vanishing pension that disappears the minute you go to collect it." -George Carlin

So where do we go from here you may ask? Where can we turn? How were smart people educated before this piece of shit Prussian system got rammed down our throats? The founding fathers were pretty damn smart, how were they educated? Those Greeks and Romans were pretty damn smart too. How were they educated? The Renaissance artists and scholars, how about them? They were products of the Classical Education System.

Classical Education

There may be a better way to educate our kids it called the Classical Education or the Classical Liberal Arts Education. Liberal in this sense has nothing to do with Liberal as it is denoted in today's crazy political world. The word liberal keeps changing forms, it's the Bruce Jenner of words. In centuries past it was synonymous with liberty, individual freedom, and being well informed. Now it means you want the state to fix all your problems and take care of you. You see the word started out as a rugged dude and ended up a spoiled middle aged woman.

Within this context liberal comes from the Latin word "liber" which is defined as "free man" or "suitable for a free man". Art is from the Latin word "artem", this has nothing to do with kids standing around with paint brushes all day or beating on bongo drums. It means work of art, practical skill, a business, a craft. So what Liberal Arts Education means is "free man practical skill." In the ancient Rome it was outlawed to teach this "free man" education to slaves. I wonder fucking why? Is it because they'll start thinking for themselves? It's hard to push a population of people around who have critical thinking skills and have been formally trained in logic. It's a bad place to be when people start thinking for themselves when you are in charge and have been a dick. This "free man practical skill" system has produced the greatest minds in history. In 1999 A&E cable network broadcast a list of "The 100 Most Influential People of the Past 1000 years." This was when the Arts and Entertainment Network wasn't a complete pile of programming shit before it's decent into mindless reality programming hell. The list of the top 10 influential names in the last 500 years was put together by scholars.

1. Johann Gutenberg
2. Isaac Newton
3. Martin Luther
4. Charles Darwin
5. William Shakespeare
6. Christopher Columbus
7. Karl Marx
8. Albert Einstein
9. Copernicus
10. Galileo

A very curious group of people. We have a writer, a theologian, a philosopher, an inventor, and five scientists. Some from various religions and some atheists. What is the one common thread between these people? They all had a classical education.

Classical education has a history of over 2500 years in the Western world. It began in Greece, was adopted by the Romans. It faltered after the fall of Rome during the Dark ages. During the

Italian Renaissance it made its resurgence. This education system then passed to England, and then to America. During the establishment of the US, classical education was thriving. Thomas Jefferson, probably one of the smartest of the founding fathers recommended classical education. These founders would reference classics like Plutach's lives of the noble Greeks and Romans in their conversations. It gave the population common ground which created the early American cultural fabric based upon individual independence. Americans loved and respected George Washington because he exhibited the qualities of the Roman patriot Lucius Quinctius Cincinnatus. Who was this Cincinnatus?

He was lived around 500 B.C., and was such a bass-ass Cinncinnati Ohio was named in his honor. That's some staying power folks. He was regarded as one of the early heroes of early Rome and was a role model of virtue and simplicity. When his son was convicted and condemned to death, he was forced to live by humble means, working his small farm, until an invasion caused him to be called to serve Rome as dictator. Two weeks after defeating the invasion and the end of the crisis he stepped down from his role of near-absolute authority. He has often been cited as an example of outstanding leadership, service to the greater good, civic virtue, lack of personal ambition, and modesty. In many ways paralleling the traits of George Washington. Now compare this great example of leadership to the fuck-sticks that have been presidents and in congress over the last few decades. It's disgusting.

Classical education has played a fundamental role of education in the West. Without it, there would be no West. What was it about this educational system that so captivated and shaped the Western world?

1. Classical education values knowledge for its own sake.

2. It upholds the standards of correctness, logic, beauty, and truth all intrinsic to the Liberal Arts.
3. Classical education demands moral virtue of its followers.
4. It prepares its citizens to resume responsibility in the political order.

As a system of education that values knowledge for its own sake it breaks from the current system which only promotes schooling as preparation for adult work. Or learning just to pass a tests. The premise of the classical education starts with the idea that humans are thinking creatures which are curious and want to know objective truth.

If you pay attention to kids one of the first questions they ask is "what is it"? They want to know and understand their surroundings? Wouldn't it make sense in a system of education to take advantage of people's built-in curiosity? Knowledge does not come to humans unaided by nature. Children naturally have the tools to understand the world around them, but they need direction. When kids are young they have a lot more mental capabilities then we give them credit. Think how easily they pick up language and absorb information. There is an enormous amount of potential brain power that classical education taps into. Rather than denying biology and boxing in the mind as in the Prussian system, it harnesses biology for the best outcome.

A child's brain is rapidly growing, constantly changing, and making billions of connections between various parts of the brain. A human at any age has about 100 billion neurons. The synapse in the brain is the connection point between two neurons. An adult has about 300 billion connections and a child has about a quadrillion connections. We are born with about 100 billion neurons but those quadrillion connections haven't been made yet. These connection are formed at a very rapid pace during the first 5 years of life, at 700-1000 new synapses per second. These connections are created through every interaction a child has and are extremely important because they form the architecture of the brain.

Every interaction with a child, the brain is growing, connecting different parts of the brain. This promotes new ideas, insights, and creative thinking. More interaction equals more connections. During these early years, a child's brain makes as many connections as possible. Then the brain starts to abandon the connections that are not being used and strengthening the ones that are used. This a process that continues throughout life. This process is known as synaptic plasticity, the ability of a synapses to straighten or weaken over time, in response to increased or decreased activity. The difference between a dumb-ass and a genius in large part is due to synaptic plasticity.

A kid's brain is activated by everything he or she experiences, it can also be overwhelmed. This causes stress and the body's alarm system activates. This is a simple survival mechanism. Stress=bad=avoid. If the stress is taken away the brain goes back to normal. While dealing with stress is part of life, situations that cause stress during development are going to have a deep impact. The Prussian structured Common Core education system manufactures stresses and artificial compartmentalization of information. This will cause synaptic pruning which will impact creative and critical thinking that will have lifelong consequences. Could the synapsis' that are used for learning and the abstract reasoning ability (divergent thinking) be weakened while strengthening the connections for fear and submission? This process causes compartmentalization of thoughts and perceptions. The brain has the ability to change throughout life, however, these early formative years are fundamental in building a strong foundation for creativity, curiosity, and intelligence. I guess the question is do we want let nature help us out to create beautiful thinking people or do we manufacture robot people? Over 150 years ago in Prussia, Wundt developed the educational process we use today to inhibit thinking by creating stimuli in children's learning environment to "modifiability in the path of neural conduction" when people are young.

This neurology plays directly into divergent thinking. Professor Sir Kenneth Robinson described divergent thinking (abstract reasoning ability) as, "It's the ability to see lots of possible answers to a question, lots of possible ways to interpret a question, to think laterally, to think not just in linear or convergent ways, to see multiple answers, not one." In a study for divergent thinking 98% of Kindergarten children tested at the "genius" level, suggesting that every child has the capacity for divergent thinking. Their neurological development supports this premise. However, when divergent thinking tests were repeated with the same children five years later, and five years after that, the percentage of students performing at the "genius" level dropped greatly each time. Sadly dropped to the point very few still had the capacity to think divergently ten years after the first test.

Robinson believes the reason why student's ability for divergent thinking diminishes as they get older is due to the fact, "it's pretty much taught out of them. They've spent ten years at school, being taught there's only one answer." There is little or no reward for divergent thinking in our world of standardized to the test model of schooling. It's effectively giving people's minds tunnel vision, rather than seeing how all the tunnels interconnect.

In recent years a lot of development has gone into brain scans to identify problems with the brain. Doctors such as Dr. Daniel Amen is one of the early pioneers for using brain scans to identify various mental issues. He's applying sound logic to his area of psychiatry which implies mental issues are from networking errors in the brain. He wants to see the network, and how it's functioning before, during, and after treatment. What he has found with people having behavior problems is striking. A lot of these people are suffering from neurological connection errors. This idea of brain scanning has also moved into Functional Magnetic Resonance Imaging of the human brain which maps the brain communicating with different parts of itself.

A recent study by Yale University entitled, *Functional connectome fingerprinting: identifying individuals using patterns of brain connectivity.* What they found was very interesting. People with high brain connectivity have higher ability to abstract reason or in other words think divergently. "The more certain regions are talking to one another, the better you're able to process information quickly and make inferences," says Emily Finn, a grad student at Yale one of the authors of the study. A strong connection between the frontal and parietal lobes, especially, meant a high fluid intelligence score. Both regions are involved in high-level mental function, Finn says, which makes sense: "They kind of underpin all of the sophisticated stuff that makes us humans to begin with." *Wired, 10.12.15, Scientist Can Now Predict Intelligence From Brain Activity.*

So, let use our connections between our frontal and parietal lobes for a moment, and do some thinking. Assuming the following 4 following items, maybe we can make sense of the situation.

1. We know the framework of education system was created in large part by the German mad scientist Dr. Wundt and grandaddy of Nazism Johann Fitche to make people stupid by intentionally screwing with the natural development of the

brain by how people are taught in school. At this point in history, it's a safe assumption all mad scientists come from Germany.

2. We have reached peak stupid in our country, and education is a huge problem, and it seems everything is talked about except the structure of the system itself.

3. According to Professor Robinson, 98% of kindergarteners have genius level abstract reasoning ability (divergent thinking). This ability decreases over time because it appears this vital skill is taught out of children.

4. fMRI scans have now linked abstract reasoning ability (divergent thinking) to connectivity of the brain within itself by resonance image mapping. Given the available data and as long as the technology can handle what we are demanding for testing, we can scientifically prove our school system is making us stupid, or basically giving us low grade brain damage. Two studies would be required. Would we be ready for the results, and would we accept the science?

First study. Professor Robinson or someone like him, team up with some of the people from Yale and conduct his same study with the addition of fMRI technology. One set of kids tested from the Prussian system and one from classical liberal arts system. They would be able to track the cognitive ability of the children in reference to abstract reasoning ability (divergent thinking) over time. Second test. Conduct a study of teenage or young adults from similar backgrounds, households, grade point levels, drug use etc. with the major differing factor of education type, Prussian system vs. Classical Liberal Arts Education. I'm not a betting man, but if I owned a farm I would bet on the following hypothesis.

First test would show declines over the years in abstract reasoning ability (divergent thinking) in proctored tests and fMRI results would show a decline in connectivity in brain mapping more severely in the Prussian system educated group than the Classical Education Group.

Second test would show students with the Classical Liberal Arts Education would test better in abstract reasoning ability (divergent thinking), and their fMRI mapping will be more active than their Prussian system educated friends. A test of this importance, showing these result should result in a Nobel Prize because of its far reaching implications. Imagine that, scientific proof that an education system designed for liberated or "free minded" people being healthier for the brain. Seems like a common sense conclusion, maybe nature could be telling us something.

However, funding would be tricky because it would undermine a host of academic ideologies. It would also call in to question the history of the public education system promoted by the most powerful people in the world. Hopefully, someone has the balls to definitively prove without a shadow of a doubt how fundamentally flawed our education system is. I would love to transition to a career in neuroscience. I have a feeling a lot of our societal and economic problems could be sorted out by closer examination of the function of human brain. Such a movement is underway, with the advent of neuroeconomics. There's no fixing a problem without first identifying the problem. All signs and everything I have researched on this topic point to this conclusion, the system is fundamental messed up. I could be wrong, I hope I'm wrong, but I doubt it. The reality of the situation is really fucked up. I'm sure I'm not the only one who has made this hypothesis.

So how does this classical method of learning leverage the natural brain power of our kids? It incorporates the Trivium method of learning, it's been around a long time. The Trivium method of learning is comprised of Grammar, Logic, and Rhetoric. We know for certain it was around during ancient Greece. Some claim or suppose it may have even come from ancient Egypt as a learning/teaching method because most of the great Greek philosophers studied in Egypt. Quick note, Rhetoric does not mean Rhetoric as it is normally defined today. Rhetoric in this sense means the application of knowledge into form, writing, talking, etc.

The poor English language has been so bastardized before long, up will mean down, and hot will mean cold. There are three stages of learning. Grammar is taught in the lower school where the tools of thought are being learned - the raw data. Logic is taught in the next stage, junior high, which is the understanding stage - data processing. The last stage is the high school is Rhetoric phase where the focus is on application and communication - data output. All these processes integrate with how a child's brain naturally develops as just explained.

In the Grammar Stage, kids are able to memorize information extremely easily. They are sponges, ever noticed how fast they pick up a curse word you may not wanted them to hear? During this stage, as much information is packed into learning through songs, rhymes, chants, etc. Things that kids don't get tired of repeating. Notice how your kids can watch the same damn movie, or hear the same bed time story over and over again. The more engaging the process the better. In this stage kid's start learning the classics. The classics have stood the test of time, and are the best stories to pass down. The classics are the wisdom of the ages. Wouldn't it make sense for everyone to inherit this wisdom? Another subject that is taught in this stage is Latin. Some may think why the hell do you need Latin? Well, for one it's the foundation of all the Romance languages and about 65% of English is from Latin. However, more importantly it helps you know your own native language better. As a result a lot more thought is applied to word definitions, and language is understood as a system. I fundamental element of success in society is the ability communicated effectively. Also, kids who learn Latin test better on standardized testing. Once you've learned one foreign language it's easier to learn others, especially when it's a root language. This is extremely import because it teaches people meanings of words, and this is further built upon when the children get older and learn logic. This is the difference between being a wordsmith and a word user.

The approach taken in teaching history is done in a chronological order, from ancient to modern sequentially multiple times. This promotes a contextual understand of our place in history, and an understanding of the past which is critical to move past societal mistakes. Primary documents are used when possible rather than text books. This gives people the opportunity to form their own thoughts on historical events rather than told what to think. It gives the student an opportunity to put themselves into that place in history, and offers context to the world which surrounds them.

Logic is the next phase of development which happens in junior high. This age is when children naturally start to apply some of their own thinking and become a pain in the ass. As a parent, they start to use logic against you to get what they want. They really want to know how and why. Instead of quelling this normal attribute of development, the classical method harnesses it. These kids start to do their own research, and compare contrast exercises to strengthen critical thinking. The focus is on creating activities that will create a deep understanding of the subject they are learning. A test based learning system is the lowest form of learning, you don't remember squat. It's remembering and forgetting. How many episodes of Jay Leno's "Jay Walking" or youtube videos do we have to watch to figure out people don't know shit? Also during this period of time kids take classes in formal logic. They are exposed to and learn the various logical fallacies. If this skill alone was drilled into people's heads, this class alone would put crooked politicians and conmen for the most part out of business.

Finally the High School Rhetoric phase, kids with the acquired tools and information in the last two phases synthesize the information to form their own opinions and communicate those ideas in an effective manner. This is the culmination of the classical education. They are given chances to discuss and analyze their ideas which will foster an even deeper understanding of the world around them. During this time they are given years of education in writing and speaking articulately. It gives children the frame work of how to learn effectively which propagates into adulthood. They are armed with: history, logic, mathematics, science, and the ability to think for themselves. This thinking mechanism of input, process, and output is developed. Not until the logical processing portion of the thinking has been accomplished is there any strong opinions made. As patterned based emotional thinkers, we tend to jump to a lot of conclusions without doing much thinking. Or we hold certain opinions that are easily proven wrong. Most of us are not armed with formal logic training.

Classical education leads to cultural literacy. According Yale professor Ed Hirsh, cultural literacy refers to the "reservoir of common facts, ideas, and references that a group of people must possess to communicate ideas effectively". How much cultural literacy is being propagated in the current education system? Not much if the state of our current economy, politics, and incarceration rates are any indicator.

From what history has shown, only a culturally literate country can live up to the demands of freedom. The amount of people who are cultural literate seems to be shrinking, as a result we see the rise of the cultural literate comedian pointing out the follies society by the use of reason. Beneath the humor lies a layer of social commentary that seems to be one of the only voices of reason that sees the light of day. Socrates believed democracy could not survive without wise and virtuous citizens. How could it be any other way? Dr. Martin Luther King Jr. a student of the classics had the following to say about education.

"Intelligence plus character - that is the true goal of education." - Martin Luther King, Jr

A classical education should be the birthright of every child. Imagine if more people had an opportunity in this kind of educational system. An educated populous that knew their history so deeply they'd be less likely to repeat the mistakes of the past. This fundamental knowledge base lead to this great country, a fact lost on the vast majority of Americans. We would have a citizenry that would base their opinions off reason rather than folly or emotion. Can you imagine people who understand logically fallacies, and knew when they heard them? The deception by the media would top. The deception by politicians would stop because it would no longer be tolerated. The deception by capital interests would stop. People would be able to spot bull shit from a mile away rather than continuing to be manipulated. CNN, FOX News, and MSBC would lose all their viewers or be forced to fundamentally change how they relay information. An enlightened population would emerge.

One of the people that pinned the tail on the donkey dealing with education problems mentioned earlier is John Taylor Gatto. He is a former school teacher for nearly 30 years in New York City. He taught both rich and poor. During his teaching years he tried to identify by investigating deeply what works vs what doesn't work. I suggest reading his books, or at the very least google his name and do some research. What he says is logical, and should be Common Sense. In his investigation he studied the elite schools. These elite schools are were the people pushing common core (Gates, Bushes, Clintons etc.) send their children to learn. You really think they are going to dumb down their own kids? He noticed 14 themes in their curriculum that he introduced into his own classroom. As a result he was named New York City Teacher of the Year in 1989, 1990, 1991, and New York State Teacher of the Year in 1991. The kids in his classroom excelled, and it wasn't due to more money being spent, or federalized standardization of testing and curriculum. Here's the list of themes of the elite schools:

14 Themes:

1. A theory of human nature (as embodied in history, philosophy, theology, literature and law).
2. Skill in the active literacy (writing, public speaking).
3. Insight into the major institutional forms (courts, corporations, military, education).
4. Repeated exercises in the forms of good manners and politeness; based on the truth that politeness and civility are the foundation of all future relationships, all future alliances, and access to places that you might want to go.
5. Independent work.
6. Energetic physical sports are not a luxury, or a way to "blow off steam," but they are absolutely the only way to confer grace on the human presence, and that that grace translates

into power and money later on. Also, sports teach you practice in handling pain, and in dealing with emergencies.

7. A complete theory of access to any place and any person.

8. Responsibility as an utterly essential part of the curriculum; always to grab responsibility when it is offered and always to deliver more than is asked for.

9. Arrival at a personal code of standards (in production, behavior and morality).

10. To have a familiarity with, and to be at ease with, the fine arts (cultural capital).

11. The power of accurate observation and recording. For example, sharpen perception by being able to draw accurately.

12. The ability to deal with challenges of all sorts.

13. A habit of caution in reasoning to conclusions.

14. The constant development and testing of prior judgments: you make judgments, you discriminate value, and then you follow up and "keep an eye" on your predictions to see how far skewed, or how consistent, your predictions were. Critical thinking.

We throw away billions on common core, and ignore these 14 themes. If the elite are getting this life training, why aren't we? This is what promotes "non-cognitive" skills, or what I refer to is human thinking skills. Why are they receiving a Liberal Art Education, "Free-man" arts education system that liberates the mind of the individual? But we get a system that presents incoherent ensemble of force memorized information which leads to emotional and intellectual dependence? Instead of being led by the voice of reason and understanding the meaning of real intellectual freedom, we are pushed around by our ideologies, manipulated by emotion, and dependent upon authority. Self-confidence is knocked down, trusting your own mind becomes an emotional driven endeavor, and you're forced to look to others to do your thinking and problem solving for you. The result of this intellectual vacuum has resulted in a population of people lashing out at misperceived threats to their feelings in the form of a rampant PC culture and general discontent. If you don't believe in freedom of expression for people you hate, you don't believe in freedom at all. It can in no way otherwise exist.

Society without constructive dialog is nothing more than crabs in a boiling pot pulling each other down. The only way to evolve as a society is for individuals one at a time start thinking for themselves, otherwise the thinking will be done for you. Reaching ones potential is made extremely difficult when the ability to actualize one's potential has never been fostered, but it's never too late to start thinking for yourself and questioning.

"It's very important to help people figure out how to manage life, to help people figure how to think, help inspire them, help show them what can be gained from setting goals and achieving them and that excellent feeling - and that it becomes contagious. Then you can do more with that - you can inspire other people, you can surround yourself with a bunch of likeminded people, and instead of being jealous of each other, actually elevate each other and grow strong as a group then you would as individuals. There are a lot of things people just don't get to learn. And sometimes you're around the wrong people, you have the wrong job, you have the wrong career, you have the wrong whatever and you never get around those people. And then one day you're old as fuck and you realize you wasted your life doing shitty things that are boring, hanging around with assholes who have no social skills, nobody elevated anybody and then your fucking ticker stops. It's a tragedy. I don't think that aspect of society is necessary. I really feel like it is a mismanaged

resource issue. Human beings are a resource. A life is a resource." -
Joe Rogan

Interesting Material:

Wired.com - *Scientist Can Now Predict Intelligence From Brain Acitivity*. 11.12.15

Yale University, *Functional connectome fingerprinting: identifying individuals using patterns of brain connectivity. Interdepartmental Neuroscience Program*. 2015

Gatto, John Taylor. *The Underground History of American Education*. Odysseus Group. 2000

Gatto, John Taylor. *Dumbing Us Down: The Hidden Curriculum of Compulsory Schooling*. New Society Publishers. 2002.

Jospeh, Miriam. *The Trivium: The Liberal Arts of Logic, Grammar, and Rhetoric*. Paul Dry Books. 2002.

Chapter 4

The Media

"The media's the most powerful entity on earth. They have the power to make the innocent guilty and to make the guilty innocent, and that's power. Because they control the minds of the masses". – Malcom X

Media is simply the means of communication. Radio, television, newspaper, movies, and internet are all forms of media which transmits data which molds our thoughts, and our perceptions of reality. Information and ideas are the most powerful influences in the molding society. Edward Bulwer-Lytton knew this when he coined the phrase, "The pen is mightier than the sword". Understanding that pen represents ideas which control the use of swords is import to understand when looking at our media, and its ability to motivate people. Modern media has been around for over 100 years. Critical to understanding our modern media, we need know its past. One of the most underrated, but extremely influential people who's lived in the last 100 years is named Edward Bernays. In fact, ideas and teachings created by Bernays affects us day in and day out without most of us realizing this fact.

Edward Bernays is the father of propaganda, later renamed Public Relations and Advertising. The Nazi's ruined the word propaganda because of the information they were spreading. Thus, it's now it's become a pejorative word. The news media should be a platform to disseminate unbiased information that gives insight into what is going on in the world. However, this is too powerful of a tool to leave alone. It's the power to influence public sentiment and thinking. As the nephew of Sigmund Freud, Bernays incorporated Freud's psychoanalytical ideas to influence the masses. He believed that inside of each person, and especially the masses was an irrational and dangerous being that needs to be manipulated to insure safety. He believed decision making, and therefore accurate information without spin is only for the elite running society. He believed in a enlighten despotism which would control society beyond public scrutiny.

During World War I, Bernay's worked for Woodrow Wilson on the Committee on Public Information. The public had always been reluctant to go to war for obvious reason, war is incredibility expensive and getting shot or blown up sucks. Bernays was influential in promoting the idea that America was "bringing democracy to all of Europe". As Americans we love the idea of democracy, even though we have become an oligarchy. Traditionally, we have thought that everyone should have it because of the freedoms we once enjoyed. Even after 100 years we are still banging on the drum of democracy to enforce our will, while we don't enjoy a democratic society ourselves. Ironic. Bernays wondered if this model of propaganda could be used in peacetime to motivate people. Shortly after the war he opened a Public Relations firm which would serve as a catalyst to institutional government lying, birth of consumer culture, and news media corruption.

In 1924, President Coolidge was suffering from unpopular polls and low public sentiment. He employed Berneys to help fix his image. Berneys, understanding how people think invited 34 film stars to be entertained by Coolidge at the White House. This event was run as a story in all the newspapers across the country. This PR parlor trick improved Coolidge's opinion. This same tactic is still used to this day to endear the gullible to politicians. It's ludicrous to think actors' opinions are more valid than your own unless they are going to explain their reasoning. A similar PR move was done recently when a bunch of Hollywood actors were trotted out to speak about the nuclear deal with Iran. You have to ask yourself what the fuck does Jack Black and Morgan Freeman have to do with nuclear proliferation in Iran? Absolutely nothing is the answer, except as political move to sway people's opinion. It has nothing to do with informing people with real information.

Quickly, Burneys recognized that he could influence people to buy more goods by influencing their unconscious mind. He believed that a consumer based democracy was a happy and docile

74

democracy because people would spend all their time working focused on buying stuff. Instead of replacing things when they wore out, a consumer mentality was built. He thought material goods would act as a medication to any feeling of discomfort found in society. This concept would maintain the relationship of power of a relatively few wealthy ruling over the masses. All the while the masses are feeding into this power structure by its willingness to keep consuming at ever increasing levels. This is the psychology behind the rat race. We are all chasing that piece of cheese, and never feel satisfied. Without recognizing it we are feeding into the bread and circus idea established in Rome. Our attention is being pulled from what's important and refocused on the trivial and in a lot of cases the absurd. There are really very few new ideas in history. Just repackaged, given a new name, and reused.

*"The conscious and intelligent manipulation of the organized habits and opinions of the masses is an important element in democratic society. Those who manipulate this unseen mechanism of society constitute an invisible government which is the true ruling power of our country. ...**We are governed, our minds are molded, our tastes formed, our ideas suggested, largely by men we have never heard of.** This is a logical result of the way in which our democratic society is organized. Vast numbers of human beings must cooperate in this manner if they are to live together as a smoothly functioning society. ...In almost every act of our daily lives, whether in the sphere of politics or business, in our social conduct or our ethical thinking, **we are dominated by the relatively small number of persons...who understand the mental processes and social patterns of the masses. It is they who pull the wires which control the public mind."** - Edward Bernays*

What Bernays found was an effective way to hack democracy. A way of manufacturing consent of the masses. Since the idea of democracy rests upon the public making decisions; available information is extremely import. If it was possible to control what information the public saw you would have the ability to control how the public thinks. The tool to make this happen is Public Relations or propaganda. It's really quite simple when it's broken down. Propaganda in a democracy is the first level of controlling people. The second level is violence.

Manufacturing of consent is the ability of powerful people to influence not only what you do but what think. If you are only given a certain set of data you are only able to think in terms within that set of data. We are products of our environment in most cases. The other underlying idea is influencing people by manipulating their unconscious mind by appealing to their emotions to have them react irrationally. Therefore, how we weight information in our decision making becomes extremely important in our thinking. We may hear a message over and over again which will create a thought pathway of cognitive ease which does not properly weight various data points in our thinking.

Propaganda, Fruit, and War

In 1954, Edward Bernays would turn at complete lie into action for political and economic gain. United Fruit Company owned massive quantities of land in Guatemala, and had been supporting a series of dictators. They were concerned about the new Guatemalan president. This new president, Jacobo Arbenz, was a democratically elected socialist. United Fruit Company was unhappy about the president's policy of giving land to the people. Less than 3% of the landowners held more than 70% of the land. They nationalized more than 1.5 million acres including land held by the president's family

76

and turned it over to the peasants. United Fruit Company and a small amount of elites were unhappy with this development and hired Bernays to try to undo what was going on in Guatemala. President Arbenz was extremely popular with the people. He had given the people a means to support themselves and hope to climb from poverty.

Bernays played into the growing fear of communism, even though President Arbenz had no ties to Soviet Russia. Bernays and the Fruit Company found a top Latin-American politician to condemn the actions of President Arbenz. Burnays created a fake news agency called the Middle America Information Bureau. Their task was to pump out propaganda pieces that were picked up by major news agencies to insight fear into Americans that Guatemala was becoming the new base of Soviet operations at their back door. This was all fiction, but it worked. Via lobbying the Eisenhower administration a plot was formed to secretly topple the Arbenz government. One close look at the administration shows a huge conflict of interest. A who's who list of people from the politically powerful Council on Foreign Relations (CFR). Later in the book we will look more into the CFR. For now, suffice it to say it's the real movers and shakers of economic, military, and political policy in the US. Secretary of State John Dulles (CFR), and his brother CIA Director Allen Dulles (CFR), both had been legal counsel for United Fruit for decades. General Robert Cutler (CFR), head of the National Security Council was the former Chairman of the Board of United Fruit.

The CIA operation was named PBSUCCESS. They recruited rebels, armed them, trained them, and provide air support from the CIA. They found a leader and went to work toppling the popularly elected government for corporate interests. Leading the CIA operation was Howard Hunt, "What we wanted to have was a terror campaign. To terrify Arbenz particularly, and his troops as much as possible. As the German Stuka bombers terrified the population of Holland, Belgium, and Poland on the onset of World War II and render everyone paralyzed." Even though Guatemala was a capitalist country with no ties to Russia because of the propaganda fear campaign Americans supported this banana war.

Had the US public known the truth, the support would have been minimal. As a result, Guatemala had been thrown in to decades of terminal with hundreds of thousands of deaths. All due to corporate greed, and some fucking bananas. This ought to serve as a lesson to us today. How naive to believe this same bullshit isn't happening as you read this. Ignore what is being said on the media, look at what the real power brokers are saying, and see who is benefiting. Chances are if they were lying then. They are spinning fiction and peddling it as fact now. Iraq, Libya, Afghanistan, Syria all follow this same play book.

With this formula of influence in mind, let's take a look at some of the other work of Bernays. In the 1920's one of Edward Bernays clients was the American Tobacco Corporation. At the time there was a taboo against women smoking in public. The president of the American Tobacco Corporation saw he was losing out on 50% percent of his potential market. Bernays hired a psychologist to figure out why. The psychologist came to the conclusion that cigarettes was a symbolic form of male power over women.

Women could undermine this power by smoking themselves! It was viewed as a form of women's rights. To change the public's opinion, Bernays was able to convince a group of rich debutantes to pull out their cigarettes during the Easter Parade in New York City. Bernays informed the newspaper beforehand that these women were

78

going to be protesting for women's rights, and he knew the media would show up. When the media showed up, the women lighted up and had a banner reading "Torches of Freedom". The story was published around the world in newspapers the next day. The taboo of women smoking was broken in one event. Soon smoking by women was molded into a symbol of power for women.

In reality smoking has nothing to do with somebody's independence or empowerment. This notion lived on for decades as teenagers would smoke in a form of independence and defiance. The only thing smoking does is gives you a nicotine buzz, and increase your chances of a life ending diseases. Appealing to people's emotions by both subtle and powerful methods making them feel powerful, sexy, fearful, etc. the thinking and actions of the masses are manipulated.

Soon after the sky rocketing sales of cigarettes to women the business world took note of Bernays' success. Businesses at the time depended on rationality in promoting their goods and services. The products were marketed according to their merits and utility purpose. People normally used things until they were worn out, and then purchase a replacement because it fit its purpose. The new line of influence would appeal to emotional desires.

Cars would no longer be sold because they were reliable or worked well, but marketed because they would give a driver a sense of: freedom, being a real man, being sexy, being rich, or luxury. In short buy this, and you'll be valued by society or it will make you happy. This is leveraging man's primal instinct to be accepted and loved by the tribe. This is where keeping up with the Jones was instilled into the American psyche. As a result, America shifted from a needs culture to a desires culture. We see this manifest in the dichotomy in how businesses and families operate. Businesses normally function rationally along tight needs based operating constraints, whereas households operate normally along the lines of irrational spending. As a result of such influence, people have been trained to desire and want new things before the old are worn out or consumed. Desires overshadow needs as a result, and a consumer culture is born.

This way of life is pervasive, think back to the last time you moved and how much shit you have you don't use or you even remember buying. There is weird emotional attachment to things we can't throw out that we probably won't ever use again. The reason is because you were emotionally vested in the purchase of the items. This is manifest to the extreme on the show *Hoarders*. This consumerist mind set has been molded by people running PR campaigns has turned most people into low grade hoarders as a result. I'm guilty of it. The average household has over 300,000 items. That is a ton of shit! Currently, people are starting to wake up to the fact emotionally investing into consumer goods leads to an empty way of life.

"By the way, if anyone here is in marketing or advertising...kill yourself. Thank you. Just planting seeds, planting seeds is all I'm doing. No joke here, really. Seriously, kill yourself, you have no rationalization for what you do, you are Satan's little helpers. Kill yourself, kill yourself, kill yourself now. Now, back to the show. Seriously, I know the marketing people: 'There's gonna be a joke comin' up.' There's no fuckin' joke. Suck a tail pipe, hang yourself...borrow a pistol from an NRA buddy, do something...rid the world of your evil fuckin' presence." -Bill Hicks

Another example of propaganda in advertising Bernays pulled off launched bacon to breakfast dominance. In 1925, he was hired by Beech-Nut Packing Company to boost their bacon business.

In those days eating a small breakfast was customary, and bacon was not consider a popular breakfast food. Maybe some coffee and a piece of toast. Normally people were not eating much in the morning. Bernays knew that doctors influenced thinking and eating patterns. He wanted doctors to publicly state that eating bacon and eggs in the morning was good for you. He knew that a large number of people would follow the advice of their doctor due to the authoritative or expert respect place upon them by society. A doctor signified health which in turn means living well and a long life. Bernays sold more bacon, not by telling Americans the bacon is delicious and should be eaten at every meal like I would have suggested.

He performed a poll on 5000 doctors asking the loaded question: "Is it more healthy to eat a hearty breakfast or a skimpy breakfast?" The doctors responded with an overwhelming majority that hearty is better. The bacon advertisement then went on to say, "Nine out of ten doctors recommend a hearty breakfast" with a photo of bacon and eggs. A lot of the ads appeared to be public health advisements more than ads. Housewives of this era took this type of information very seriously and the sale of bacon skyrocketed.

Message churning, burning, and suffering.

When we cut through all the convoluted bullshit of the media with reason and common sense a picture of reality emerges. By fear mongering and creating a picture of doom, the media are able to convince the public into spending an insane amount of money on defense budgets because it makes us feel more secure. The defense budget would be much more accurately described if it was called the "offence budget", the name change alone would garner more public scrutiny. It doesn't take a rocket scientist to understand offence requires a lot of resources that could be better spent at home better our society.

Question: In today's geopolitical climate is a foreign country going to invade the US when we have enough nuclear bombs to destroy the world over a few times? Why isn't the media asking and exploring pertinent questions involving terrorism? Why are they not talking about how we armed the guys in the first place who are riding around in the back of Toyota pickup trucks? We've been screwing with that part of the world for a century, which tends to piss off the locals. The idea popular media promotes is that they hate us because "we have freedom" is complete horseshit, and defies logic. They hate us because we are a foreign power that keeps fucking with them. They are so desperate and pissed, the only thing left to hold onto is their idea of God, and hate. Thus the "zealot" is born. Americans felt that way about the British at the time of the Revolution. The Jews felt the same way when Rome occupied Jerusalem a couple millennia ago. Times of changed, people have not, humans will always lash out when they are being fucked with by a foreign superpower.

In the meantime, we are being screwed over financially in the name of patriotism and defense. Where's the media and the voice of reason? Common Sense has been drowned out by big money and the information we receive is always spotty or spun, and decisions are always made in secret. When the US invaded Iraq they lied their ass off about weapons of mass destruction, it was broadcast around the clock on the news, and when the dust settled nobody was held accountable for the death count and suffering caused on both sides. Why? They just laughed their way to the bank. All the while they have a hold of our collective wallet that is over $19 trillion in debt.

Due to the structure of our macro-economic system war spending is a transfer of wealth from the low and middle classes to the top.

It's very simple if we demystify the system by extracting the war drums of the media. Understanding the processes requires removing emotion from the equation, and see how the informational mechanisms work together systemically. All we have to do is apply the logic of Causality to this mess to see what emerges. Let the chips fall where they may... Causality is fundamental to everything, everywhere, without it time would not exist and nothing would ever change. It is simply cause and effect, one process (cause) connects to another process thus effecting it. War cost a lot of money so the Federal Reserve issues currency in the form of bonds which are sold by its member banks on the open market for profit. These bonds are what represents the national debt is heaped on our backs, and it's why we pay so much to the Federal Government with so little in return. This debt is subject to compounded interest. Investors and banks purchase these bonds as investments to reap the interest. This system is never taught in school nor is actively discussed in the media because it is a monumental fuck you to the American citizen.

The media never talks about the true cost of war. This newly issued national debt money, we all pay interest on, is poured into the defense industry. Companies like GE, Lockheed Martin, Boeing, Raytheon, and Northrup Grummon are given vast sums of money to do research and development and make fancy new devices for killing people. Meanwhile, large investment companies such as State Street Corporation and Capital World Investors own vast amounts of stock in banking and defense contracting companies.

What we'll find is that these large financial companies form an orgy of entangled ownership and control as pointed out in James Glattfelder's study *The Network of Global Corporate Control* which scientifically modeled the controlling power in our economy. When something beneficial is found during the R&D process which can be marketed commercially these entities holding the patents profit from exploiting the new technology. Even though we proved the "seed capital" in the form of national debt and our taxes, they get to soak up the profits. This shifts the risks and costs associated with R&D and places it squarely on the tax payer while they stand to reap the profits. It's gambling with your buddy's wallet, you can't lose, but he will. If this truly was a free market these technologies would be open source thereby entrepreneurship could flourish. The people who created the ideas in the first place could spin off and create their own enterprise rather than having it locked down by a greedy banking cabal. This is what we call "having your cake and eating it too." This technology in turn gets sold to us commercially, and profits flow to the top via commercial channels within this web of monetary control. After taking control of a foreign country by our government these same financial entities use our tax dollars to profit from rebuilding what we blew up, and set up shop exploiting the country for its natural resources while screwing over the local inhabitants. All of this is happening while our infrastructure, the basic physical structures and facilities needed for the operation of society are breaking down. We are being manipulated, and left out to dry. Are we going to wait for the media to point this out? Or are we going to see the results of the system, and how it has economically drained us to the point of almost complete economic collapse and debt servitude.

These truths are almost completely unmentioned in our main stream media. When they do broadcast a story relating to these topics it's only a small piece of the puzzle and it's normally spun. In effect, they are giving you only one dirt covered small piece of the mosaic so it's hard to put together. At this point it should come as no surprise that the "big six" media outlets control 90% of the media outlets. Controlling ownership is tied back to same tightly knit group of powerful financial firms as the military industrial war complex associated the Council on Foreign Relations.

If this conflict of interest, and manipulation was exposed for two weeks straight on the media people would start to truly understand the opportunity cost of this fucked up system. Apathy, racial tensions, religious and ideological differences would dissolve into white hot anger aimed at the establishment. The people holding the levers of power would no longer have power. Due to the discontentment of the average American, the inertia of society would change course toward the direction of individual freedom and transparency.

A perfect example of media and political collusion is illustrated by the release of Wikileaks documents. A list showing 65 mainstream reporters were working closely with the Clinton campaign. Regardless of party affiliation their job is to report the news, and create chummy relationships and pass favors. They were invited to elitist dinners with Hillary Clinton's Campaign Chairman John Podesta and Chief Campaign strategist Joel Benenson. There is also records of journalist asking for review by the campaign before articles are published. This is a huge problem regardless if it's Republican, Democrat, or the freaking Marxists party.

This mechanism is always running; however, when we get involved in a conflict this machine goes into high gear. The media starts banging out news stories to sway popular opinion. More money is thrown into military spending, and we are off to the races. Hollywood starts churning out movies such as Argo, Zero Dark Thirty, or American Sniper with CIA involvement. Yes, the CIA has offices in Hollywood and does consult on films and scripts. These movies have a geopolitical agenda. They are making a case for support of continued war efforts, and molding of the public's perceptions. Never broadcast loudly are the economic or business side of the story. Neither does this side of the story end up in history books we are taught from in school.

The old adage of "don't bit the hand that feeds you" rings true when it comes to journalism in the 21st century. Real investigative journalism is all but dead except from independent news sources. What do you expect? The establishment owned media to expose itself to the domestic population? No, they want us uniformed and confused. The only way to proceed with global hegemony that only benefits the elite is for us to be kept in the dark and uninformed. The main reason for such a large military intelligence is not to protect the US citizens. It is to protect the interests of the ruling elite from foreign enemies, and the domestic population. We, the US law abiding citizens are the domestic enemy. Knowledge is power, and that is why we are kept in the dark. That is the reason for so much secrecy, and spun news media. This is the reason members of Congress are kept in the dark about what our "shadow government" is doing. Think about that, elected members of Congress who represent us are kept completely kept in the dark about what goes on in our government. With all this secrecy who keeps the executive branch of the government in check? The fact that government has been in cahoots with the media was nicely illustrated in 1975.

This was exposed in House Intelligence Committee Hearing, also known as the Church Committee named after Senator Frank Church (D-ID). During the hearing, the then CIA Director William Casey (CFR) admitted that CIA creates and uses disinformation against the American people.

"I thought that it was a matter of real concern that planted stories intended to serve a national purpose abroad came home and were circulated here and believed here because this would mean that the CIA could manipulate the news in the United States by channeling it through some foreign country". - Senator Frank Church (D-ID)

When question at the House Intelligence Committee hearing this is how CIA Director William Casey (CFR) responded.

Question: *"Do you have any people being paid by the CIA who are contributing to a major circulation — American journals"*

Answer: *"We do have people who submit pieces to American journals."*

Question: *"Do you have any people paid by the CIA who are working for television networks?"*

Answer: *"This I think gets into the kind of uh, getting into the details Mr. Chairman that I'd like to get into in executive session."*

Later on when asked more questions, he responded as follows.

Question: *"Do you have any people being paid by the CIA who are contributing to the national news services — AP and UPI?"*

Answer: *"Well again, I think we're getting into the kind of detail Mr. Chairman that I'd prefer to handle at executive session."*

Current Government Secrecy and the Media

Obama administration promised to be the most transparent administration in history, but has been one of the most secretive. It's also been one of the most punitive toward whistleblowers and leakers who want to bring light to wrong doing they have observed within powerful intuitions. This administration has set a new record for stonewalling or rejecting Freedom of Information requests. It has also used an obscure federal act to prosecute whistleblowers and leakers such as: Thomas Drake, NSA whistleblower who claimed American's privacy rights were being violated; James Risen, refused to reveal sources for parts of a 2006 book in which he detailed a CIA plan to undermine Iran's nuclear program; Barret Brown, a serious journalist who has spent several years investigating the world of private surveillance and defense contractors who work hand-in-hand with the state. He was arrested and jailed in 2012, and sentence to 63 months in 2015. Taking a closer look at his case should alarm any red blooded American. The story of Barret Brown is nothing more than a shameful example of abuse of power by Government. This example of silencing free speech is emblematic of tyranny in Nazi Germany or Soviet Russia. This is freighting, and what makes it even more freighting, people are not paying attention as their liberties are being taken away. People who stand up for what is just are being punished for their moral convictions are viewed as threat to the power establishment.

"During times of universal deceit, telling the truth becomes a revolutionary act." -George Orwell

Think about how the media covers the White House regardless of who is in office. There is no real investigative journalism, only softball questions and puff pieces. Instead of dialog about important issues like murderous drone strikes in Pakistan, Yemen, Somalis, and Libya; Obama takes time to banter about with Zach Galifianakis on "Between Two Ferns". Instead of having dialog about important issues like the real economy, he spends time on a televised meeting with celebrity chef Anthony Bourdain in Vietnam. Instead of discussing solutions about the ever increasing student loan burden of young people, he goes for coffee with Jerry Seinfeld. Instead of explain why he broke his promises of ending US involvement in the Middle East, he shows up dancing on the Ellen

DeGeneres show. Instead of explain why there is less hope and change, he's playing his 300th round of golf. The President of the United States is nothing more than the propaganda spokesman of the elite, regardless of political party. They go with the globalist agenda of the elite at the determent of the US population. People who ask hard questions will not be given access. It will upset the official narrative, and their careers will suffer for it. Hence, the bullshit propaganda continues.

The collective mind of the American public has been spinning and manipulated for decades because we have been subject to nonstop propaganda on important issues and fractured by political red herrings. How do you know someone is full of shit? They don't do what they say. In the case of politics normally what is decided or done is 180 degrees from what is coming out of these peoples' mouths. Even Jesus pointed this out when he said, "Beware of false prophets, which come in sheep's clothing, but inwardly they are raving wolves. Ye shall know them by their fruits." Regardless of religious belief, this is some pretty solid advice especially when you understand the original meaning of the word prophet in Hebrew simply means "spokesman." It goes hand-in-hand with how you know when a politician is lying. Their lips are moving. If they are not doing what they said, and give no real logical explanation they are full of shit. Simple as that. Think about how this molding of perceptions works considering the next three quotes.

"The propaganda system allows the US leadership to commit crimes without limit and with no suggestion of misbehavior or criminality; in fact, major war criminals like Henry Kissinger appear regularly on TV to comment on the crimes of the derivative butchers." – Edward S. Herman Professor PhD (media analyst of corporate and regulatory issues of the political economy.)

"See, in my line of work you got to keep repeating things over and over and over again for the truth to sink in, to kind of catapult the propaganda." – George W. Bush

"Naturally, the common people don't want war, but after all, it is the leaders of the country who determine policy, and it is always a simple matter to drag people along whether it is a democracy, or a fascist dictatorship, or a parliament, or a communist dictatorship. Voice or no voice, the people can always be brought to the bidding of the leaders. This is easy. All you have to do is to tell them they are being attacked, and denounce the pacifists for lack of patriotism and exposing the country to danger. It works the same in every country." Herman Goering. (Hitler's Reich-Marshall at the Nuremberg Trails after WWII.)

The world has been propagandized into being incredibly insane that in 2009, President Obama was awarded the Noble Peace Prize. This was while the US was in two active wars. Since that time his administration has been pushing its hegemonic agenda destabilizing the whole of the Middle East via covert operations by arming mercenaries, backing Saudi's invasion of Yemen, dropping bombs from drones, and pushing us into a cold war which may turn into a hot war with Russia. Domestically, he is arguably one of the most divisive presidents in American history. That is not peace, that's anti-peace. With this same logic we should posthumously award serial murdering rapist Ted Bundy a Global Women's Rights Award. All that needs to happen is for the crazy media to say he was a hero for bring rape into the forefront of discussion, and how things have improved since he brought awareness to the rape and murder of innocent women.

Politico-Media Complex

"I'll scratch your back if you scratch mine" dictating interaction between various groups emerges in what political scientist coin the "Politico-Media Complex". This is the network relationship and interactions between the state's political and ruling classes, the media industry, law, and particularly corporations - especially multinational corporations (they own the complex). What is formed is basically top down owned and controlled Ministry of Propaganda, where evoking emotion and spinning public sentiment is more important than factual reporting or helping us understand the world we live in. Due to this information distribution complex if you want to find out what is really going on you're forced to absorb: the US press, UK press, Al Jazeera, and the Russian news, like RT. Then if you are lucky you can omit the BS and come up with an educated opinion on a topic which is coherent with reality.

All Politicians both Republican and Democrat, the media, and big business have understood how to manipulate the masses for a long time as illustrated by Edward Bernays. The campaigns of Barak Obama in 2012, and Hilary Clinton in 2016 both employed a consortium of advisors which include social psychologists. A couple notables are Susan Fiske and Robert Cialdini. Cialdini. He is best known for his 1984 book on persuasion called *Influence: The Psychology of Persuasion*. It sold over 3 million copies and *Fortune Magazine* lists the book in their "75 Smartest Business Books". Cialdini's theory of influence is based on the principles of reciprocity, commitment and consistency, social proof, authority, liking, and scarcity. He is on the money when it comes to his theory influence. It's a really good book if you want to know what makes people tick. It's even a better read if you can appreciate how you as a person are influenced. In a sense it explains the algorithms of human interaction, and how those algorithms can be hacked if you are unaware.

These six principles can be utilized to make people do things that are against their own good. When these buttons are pushed people end up supporting dictators, buying shit they don't need, and making horrible life choices because decisions were not made using critical thought. What is never mentioned, is that our lovely Prussian education system set us up to be manipulated in this manner. Our ability to think big and in diverse ways was truncated when we were young by compartmentalized forced memorization. What to think comes from experts was instilled, and the ability to critically think was never properly taught. In this respect influencing the masses becomes a lot like shooting fish in a barrel.

I believe human nature for the most part is fundamentally good. We want to get along with others. We love spending time with our family and friends. We love to laugh. We yearn to find our place in society, and feel accepted and valued for what we contribute. We'll do just about anything to have these basic human qualities realized in our lives. We want to point our energy in a direction that is worth something. This theory of influence can be used for good, but it can easily exploit people's good nature and noble desires against themselves to their detriment for somebody else's gain. Improperly used, this list of principles is the tool box of the master bullshit artist. Politicians, media, and advisors are pushing these buttons constantly. A lot like learning a magic trick, when you understand these principles you understand how the trick is played.

Six Principles of Persuasion

1. **Reciprocity** - People tend to return favors. When somebody does something for us we feel on some level obligated to the

source of gesture. Reciprocity is deeply rooted in human consciousness. Almost certainly it is an adaptive quality that emerged from living groups and tribes. Helping each other out was necessary to human survival since the being of time. As a result, most of us have a built in equilibrium with the people in our lives. This is generally a good thing as it helps us keep relationships we value healthy and strong. In today's morally bankrupt political environment were corporate money and influence far outweighs the needs of the people the reciprocal relation exists between the politician and his corporate sponsors. As a result, little regard is given to reciprocal relationship between politicians and the people. In a tell all book an anonymous congressman writes, "The average man on the street actually thinks he influences how I vote. Unless it's a hot-button issue, his thoughts are generally meaningless. I'll politely listen, but I follow the money."-*Confessions of Congressman X*

2. **Commitment and Consistenc**y - We tend to take our commitments seriously. Historically, oath giving was of huge importance. Oaths are still given, but it seems they have lost some of their binding power. Under oath we see people in politics lie their asses off. Depending on the politician makes a huge difference in how the lying is covered. The outrage is mostly manufactured by the news media. We see the psychological influence in commitment when people choosing their political affiliation. They'll stay attached to the party come hell or high water no matter how much the party has changed over the years because of the feelings of consistency this provides. If the principles you adhere to fit within a political party today doesn't mean in 20 years you'll still identify with the same party if your thinking

is rooted in ideas rather than identity. For example principles of classical liberalism are completely different than what has emerged as progressive liberalism. Two completely different animals even though they share the same name. This commitment and consistency to political party keeps their power intact even when they make changes which erode the liberties of their supporters. Without thinking, people's values will change to stay consistent to their committed political party. A great example of this is comedian Adam Carolla, In the 1990's he was considered a liberal democrat by himself and everyone else. His stances on various political topics have remained more or less the same over the years. In the sea of shifting political ideologies he's now considered a "right-winger". How did that happen? It's a result of people being committed to a group of people deciding their thinking rather than a set of principles created by a critical thinking individual. People who are committed to principles or ideas versus committed to a political party are much more difficult to manipulate.

3. **Social Proof** - People will do things they see other people doing. This is the monkey see monkey do concept. People tend to conform to others around them. We see this concept at play when you got in trouble with a friend as a kid, and your mom ask, "If Billy jumped off a cliff would you?" Of course there are always outliers among the masses; however, they are a rare minority. In some cases these outlier start their own "counter culture", but the idea still holds true among the new group. In the world of politics a powerful form of social proof is endorsements. The more endorsements by people recognized as smart or experts goes a distance in convincing people to vote for a particular

candidate. Without realizing it we are relying upon perceived knowledge or expertise of the endorsers we side with. The inverse reaction happens with a politician is snubbed by an endorser. Providing fake polling data is another way to influence the electorate. The media can publish polling result showing favorable results for a candidate or initiative so people who were going to vote the other way won't bother to show up and cast their vote.

4. **Authority** - People tend to submit their thinking to authority figures. These authority figures come in various forms of experts. Political pundits, doctors, religious leaders, and even news readers are viewed as authoritative figures when it comes to political issues. Authority figures have a rich history of influencing people. When the media is trying to prove a point, they will cart out an expert. Most of the time they have something to gain by pushing their view point, normally it fits an agenda or ideology. The other reason is that they could have built their career upon a set of information they do not want to see eroded. The wonderful thing about living today is that we do not need to rely upon the opinions of people in authority. We can consider ideas, research, and critically think about what they are claiming. For the first time in history we have the world's knowledge accessible at our finger tips. If something doesn't make sense we can research it to our hearts desire. There is no reason we cannot become as well informed on an issue as many experts, and form our own ideas.

5. **Liking** - People are persuaded by people they like. For instance, I really like my wife. I'd do pretty much anything for her, good thing she is one of the most reasonable I know. A popular political example of this influence is when

politicians partner up with the Hollywood crowd. The PR crowd is very aware that having Obama show up and dance on the Ellen Degeneres show. It's going to endear him to a large portion of the public. These PR appearances have no bearing on solving problems that really matter. We hear from various Hollywood personalities relating to a host of ideas that get broadcast to us. Depending on the topic, the media will spin what the Hollywood personality said to fit their agenda. Liking is also an important consideration in choosing people who read the news. Normally really attractive people are selected because they are better liked by the public. Take Fox News for example, the studio is wall to wall hot chicks with some father figures sprinkled in. If you were to take a poll of straight men watching Fox News 20% are fully engaged in watching the news, 60% of their minds are toggling between the news and wanting to bed a newscaster, and 20% are googling the words "wardrobe malfunctions" + "Megyn Kelly" + whoever else is on the screen on their smart phones. Before you get your panties in a bunch, it's the exaggerated truth. It is the underlying reason why people who are more attractive are more successful. People are attracted to, and like beauty. It's not fair, but nothing in life is fair.

6. **Scarcity** - When something is perceived scarce people tend react, which generates demand. Scarcity is a popular tool in politics when forming public opinion because it instills fear and it threatens one's feeling of wellbeing. When jobs growth, and social services are brought up, the influence of scarcity is being felt among people. When politicians are talking about job growth they are trying to make you feel secure or in some cases insecure. All dependent of course

96

upon who is in charge of making jobs grow. Whether or not rooted in fact scarcity is used to influence. This happens regularly. When Trump speaks about bring jobs back he is playing the scarcity card because middle class jobs have become more scarce. If the politician actually does what they remains to be seen. Normally, we're let down. To a much greater extent scarcity is used in advertising. In fact we are beat over the head with it. A perfect example of this is the diamond industry. The whole industry is built upon a false scarcity which was created by the DeBeers Diamond Cartel.

PC Culture - Media Driven Narrative – Cultural Marxism

The media has almost an Alice in Wonderland quality to it. We live in a country that prides itself on Freedom of Speech, and the open market place of ideas. However, we are seeing over and over again, on issue after issue, there is a certain narrative or ideal that is forced with a ruthlessness. A bizarre self-censorship pushed by the Politico-Media Complex. This censorship of differing ideas is heading in a bad direction if personal liberties are of value to a society. Of course we haven't the sever repercussion yet, but we are seeing how corporate power is penalizing people who say things that are not within the bounds of PC Cultural Dialog. If somebody voices an opinion that is deemed politically incorrect it seems the media is the judge, jury, and executioner and the person pays with their livelihood. A perfect example of this the Seattle Mariners reserve catcher Steve Clevenger, suspended for the rest of the season without pay. He tweeted his opinion about Black Lives Matter protesters, the controversy over police shootings, and President Obama. Here are his two tweets.

"Black people beating whites when a thug got shot holding a gun by a black officer haha fucking cracks me up! Keep kneeling for the Anthem!"

"BLM is pathetic once again! Obama you are pathetic once again! Everyone involved should be locked behind bars like animals!"

Clevenger is using some hard language, obviously not supportive of BLM. However, the response is absolutely insane. Losing his job over not supporting a political movement has nothing to do with if the guy is a racist or not. What happen to the days when somebody said something shitty, and you'd think to yourself "fuck that guy", and move on with life? Also remaining to be answered is what the fuck does this have to do with playing the game of baseball? Just how far is this word policing going to go? This is only one example of a symptom of a much bigger disease, Cultural Marxism which has been driven by the media and enveloped the political spectrum.

There has been a sad death, around 30 years ago the traditional liberal class died. Pissing on the grave stone of classical liberalism is today's neoliberal Cultural Marxist calling themselves a liberal or a progressive. If words and definitions still meant anything the classical liberal has more in similar with today's libertarian than they do today's liberals. In fact, you could classify libertarians as a subset within classical liberalism. Central to classical liberalism was the idea that the core of society is the individual who has rights, and that the government for the most part should bugger off.

So how did this shift happened? It goes back to Woodrow Wilson, who was known as a "Progressive". Progressives got a bad name during WWI when Woodrow Wilson, a puppet of the establishment, was locking up dissenters for protesting government decisions, Union busting, and setting up a central bank which has been screwing every American to this day. They ended up changing their name to liberals, because the liberal ideology was viewed by people to be a good thing. Everybody likes individual rights if you value freedom. Then as time progressed this party gave the term liberals a bad name. I would consider myself a classical liberal, now I find myself more in the camp of the Libertarians even though I do not share all their ideas. A lot of thinkers are finding this happening because they value classical liberal tenets of individual liberty.

Underlying this mind fuck, is that fact this movement of Cultural Marxism pits the loons from the far right and left of the political spectrum against each other. This is what's propelling this PC culture, which leads to self-imposed censorship fueled by the Media. It's all about control, as policy maker Zbigniew Brzezinski (CFR) points out in *Between Two Ages: America's Role in the Technetronic Era.*

"In the technotronic society the trend would seem to be towards the aggregation of the individual support of millions of uncoordinated citizens, easily within the reach of magnetic and attractive personalities exploiting the latest communications techniques to manipulate emotions and control reason."

We see this all the time in the media when these personalities are telling us how we should feel or think about a news story. Here's an interesting fact, Brezezinski's daughter Mika is an attractive television personality. She is a TV personality on MSNBC's morning program *Morning Joe* where her father is a frequent guest. You can't make this shit up folks, sometimes truth is stranger than fiction.

Political Correctness - The Rise of the Sheep-Ape

American media today is dominated by a system of beliefs, attitudes and values that we have come to know as "Political

Correctness." Over the past decade we have seen political correctness go beyond reasonable to the absurd. Political Correctness is deadly serious in its aims, seeking to impose a uniformity of thought and behavior on all Americans. It is therefore totalitarian in nature. If you do not fit within the box, you have no place in the corporate sponsored media. Its roots lie in Cultural Marxism, and if you are a freethinking person, it is fucked. This is WHY examples are constantly being created in the media as sacrificial lambs to the God of Political Correctness. It's evoking fear by regulating vocabulary which in turn controls thought. This insanity has even made its way into standup comedy.

"If the freedom of speech is taken away then dumb and silent we may be led, like sheep to the slaughter." –George Washington

For Cultural Marxist culture to emerge, the existing culture must be destroyed. Architect of Cultural Marxism Georg Lukacs said, "I saw the revolutionary destruction of society as the one and only solution to the cultural contradictions of the epoch.... Such a worldwide overturning of values cannot take place without the annihilation of the old values and the creation of new ones by the revolutionaries." In 1923, Lukacs and other Marxist intellectuals founded the Institute of Social Research at Frankfurt University in Frankfurt, Germany. The Institute, which became known as the Frankfurt School. At this point in history it is safe to assume nothing good relating to educational systems, psychology, or politics comes from Germany. The Frankfurt School's studies combined the worst Germany had to offer in Marxist analysis with Freudian psychoanalysis to form the basis of what became known as "Critical Theory."

Critical Theory is essentially destructive criticism of the main elements of Western culture, including classic liberalism, classical education, Christianity, capitalism, authority, the family, tradition, sexual restraint, loyalty, patriotism, and real nationalism. Once this was destroyed a new system of thought can be installed, and manipulated. When addressing the general public, the media advocates of Political Correctness, or Cultural Marxism, present their beliefs with appealing simplicity as merely a commitment to being "sensitive" to other people. This is completely at odd with what made Western Culture great and at odds with classical liberalism. Where decent is expected, ideas are rationally discussed, and dialog is of value. Of course there were some bullshit ideas that had to go. However, in the haste of getting rid of some of the bad cultural ideas we threw the baby out with the bath water. Not unlike the over excited demolition crew important ideals have been thrown out with the waste. There is too much black and white, bipolar thinking going on. What most people do not understand, within the wreckage of Western Culture lies the most important ideal, the importance and sovereignty of the individual over the government. This is Freedom, this idea insures your children live a better life than you do, this insures a life where the pursuit is happiness is realized. We need to recognize this fact, and intellectually hold onto like the love of your life.

America is in the throes of the greatest and direst transformation in its history. That is why people who are paying attention are asking, "What the fuck is going on? Has everyone lost their god damn minds?" We are becoming an ideological state ran by a corporate oligarchy which is mowing over individual sovereignty and rights. We don't want to recognize it because we call it Political Correctness and laugh it off. However, it's not funny, it's here, it's growing and it's destroying people's careers and lives. It seeks to destroy everything that we have ever defined as our freedom, and our culture will be redefined by the corporate totalitarian oligarchy who are the true power brokers of this country. WAKE THE FUCK UP! It's already happening now.

The newest development of this PC censorship is on YouTube with what it's calling the "Heroes" program. It is giving social justice warrior's license to sensor other people. Social justice warriors for the most part are Cultural Marxist who are too stupid to self-realize what they are. It turns censorship into a game by allowing users to earn points and ascend to new levels. Once a user reaches the higher levels, they are given the power to report "inappropriate" videos, "mass flag" videos and delete comments. After 5 days this policy is so unpopular that it has received over 700,000 'thumbs down' compared with just over 18,000 'thumbs up'. The backlash was so vitriolic that YouTube has disabled the comments on the video, bitch move YouTube, bitch move. If somebody has something horrible to say, people will not listen to them. There is no need to sensor. YouTube is apparently unaware of the fact most American's hate censoring and love free speech. They must be taking tips from North Korea or China were censorship is tolerated.

This is on the heels of another unpopular move where YouTube de-monetized content they deemed controversial or insensitive. This move is not too far removed from China's new social credit system which rates each citizen's trustworthiness. If this isn't Orwellian, I don't know what is. By 2020, everyone in China will be enrolled in a vast national database that compiles fiscal and government information, including minor traffic violations, and distils it into a single number ranking each citizen. This system tracks financial and consumption actives of the users, and what they say on social media.

"Western Culture has become a tireless brigade of social-justice warriors and that being outraged and upset and feeling bullied or offended are not only things we enjoy, they're also things we have become addicted to. When we can't purposefully get our feelings hurt by a comedian, we usually find another, albeit less satisfying, source of indignation... I choose to believe that we are addicted to the rush of being offended, the idea of it, rather than believing we have become a nation of emasculated children whose only defense against an abyss of emotional agony is a trigger warning." –Jim Norton Comedian

The lunacy of the PC culture of Cultural Marxism is completely absurd and is coming out of college campuses. Jeannie Suk wrote in an online article for *The New Yorker* about law students asking her fellow professors at Harvard not to teach rape law - or, in one case, even use the word violate (as in "that violates the law") lest it cause students distress. Students are complaining about being exposed to offensive texts written by Edward Said and Mark Twain. Northwestern University professor Laura Kipnis writes, "Emotional discomfort is regarded as equivalent to material injury, and all injuries have to be remediated." This crazy culture is now putting professors' livelihoods in jeopardy because of kids making complaints because of hurt feelings.

All of this, is a simple manifestation of people having no real rudder in life, and not having the ability to critically think for themselves. This social engineering takes the critical thinking away from the individual and places it into rules and regulations of institutional and corporate bureaucracy who gets to dictate to society. This is the wet dream of any control system. This reduces the thinking human into a "sheep-ape." If these human sheep aren't kept PC happy, they revert to their ape tendencies and start throwing

103

verbal feces at all perceived threats. Fucking sheep-apes. The Urban Dictionary is correct when defines political correctness as "the way we speak in American so we don't offend whining pussies." As the British would say, "we are becoming a society ruled by the fallacious thinking of cunts."

Now think about this deeply, and how the combination of these factors play out in what we see today. We have been educated in a school system which never taught us how to critically and mindfully think, and stamped down our independence. Further reinforced with helicopter parenting has stripping away the independent nature of people, and never was given the chance to grow. We are constantly bombarded with media for the sole purpose to evoke emotion. As a result, thinking will be performed on the emotional plane of thought. People enveloped in the PC culture are relegated to nothing more than human attack dogs barking at the threats of shadows. Now YouTube wants to use these people to sensor the rest of us? Rather than giving real thought to what is actually fucked up with society, we are a culture with a debilitating case of schizophrenia. Psychiatrist Robert Skinner once said the following.

"If people can't control their own emotions then they have to start trying to control other people's behavior." Dr. Robert Skinner

Comedians Raging Against the Machine of PC Culture

Comedians are well aware of this constricting noose that is being placed around our collective necks when it comes to using words. Think about that for a minute. Using words is under attack. In many cases throughout history they have been the renegades and social critics of the American experience. Working on stage with nothing more than a microphone and their wit these artists have been

104

our critics, our conscience, and in many cases our prophets. They have been the outsider looking in, and bring light to the insanity of our culture.

"Ridicule is the only weapon which can be used against unintelligible propositions." –Thomas Jefferson

November of 2015, Douglas Belkin of *The Wall Street Journal* wrote an article *For Stand-Up Comedians, Shows on Campus Are Often No Joke* illustrates the direction of the PC lunacy. Popular comedians such as Chris Rock and even Jerry Seinfield have sworn of college campuses because the audiences are too easily offended. The schools often have contracts forbidding certain words and even topics.

The president of Fire, the Foundation of Individual Rights in Education, one of the partners in the anti-PC film titled *Can We Take a Joke* had the following to say. "The timing is perfect. The year kicked off with comedian Chris Rock saying that he did not like playing campuses anymore, and that comedy legend George Carlin didn't like to either. Now, with Jerry Seinfeld and Bill Maher condemning the oversensitivity and humorlessness of college students, the world seems ready to make a stand for comedy. The through-line of the film follows the life and career of famous iconoclastic comedian Lenny Bruce, making the argument that Lenny Bruce would not stand a minute on the modern college campus. The film also features a few important FIRE cases in which censorship tried to crush satire, parody, and comedy on campus — sometimes successfully."

The reason why comedy is such a weapon in the defense of common sense, it employs man's most potent weapon – Ridicule. This fact is brought to light in Saul D. Alinsky's book *Rules for Radicals*. Regardless of what anyone thinks about the book *Rules for Radicals* or Saul D. Alinsky, it's extremely difficult to argue against the power of ridicule. Ridicule back by witty use of reason filters out the bullshit, and lays low power and bad ideas. This is part of the reason why there has been so much comedy making fun of Hitler even though he's been dead for quite some time. Comedy and ridicule is the great leveling power because dictators and evil doers don't like to be made fun of. People in power always want to shut up people who want to criticize, one of the first places that gets attacked first are the truth tellers. Part of the reason we have an urge to ridicule these people is because on some deeper level we understand their "persona" is built from house of cards which is reinforced with bullshit.

At this point in history we won't get put in jail for telling jokes like Lenny Bruce in the 1960's. However, within the corporate oligarchy we all live, you will lose your job or livelihood if the oligarchy owned PC media police deem what you said is out of bounds. The "offensive story" will get propagated by the media, picked up by social media and outrage will spread among the people who are addicted to being outraged. How are we supposed to get to the root of problems when everyone is offended?

Political Correctness is nothing more than a form of intolerance. What the feeble minded do not understand is that it comes disguised as tolerance. It attempts to restrict the words people use with strict set of ideals dictated by today's "super liberals" or Cultural Marxists, and mob enforced by the "sheep-apes". Putting the emphasis on this red herring (PC Speech), as a society we are unable to see problems which go much deeper than the words we use. When language is being attacked, it's a symptom of something much greater, it's an attempt to deny reality to feel better or more secure. If we've gone this far off the rails in an attempt to deny reality by stifling speech, it may be a good time to open our eyes and wake up to reality.

Right now, is the time for comedians to really punch-up, and punch-up hard at the powers that be and expose the nonsense in our current situation. Ridicule backed by logic, is extremely powerful. It's time to start landing truth bombs on the problematic institutions that are crippling our society and reducing our individual freedom.

More interesting stuff to think about:

Here are some materials which are helpful in putting this crazy world into context, and most of all to provoke thought.

Books:

Bernays, Edward. *Propaganda*. Ig Publishing. 1928

> *The first lines of the book sums it up pretty well: "The conscious and intelligent manipulation of the organized habits and opinions of the masses is an important element in democratic society. Those who manipulate this unseen mechanism of society constitute an invisible government which is the true ruling power of our country."*
>
> *"Bernays' honest and practical manual provides much insight into some of the most powerful and influential institutions of contemporary industrial state capitalist democracies."—Noam Chomsky*

Chomsky, Noam. Media Control: *Second Edition: The Spectacular Achievements of Propaganda*. Seven Stories Press. 2002.

> *"Noam Chomsky's backpocket classic on wartime propaganda and opinion control begins by asserting two models of democracy—one in which the public actively participates, and one in which the public is manipulated and controlled." Not hard to guess which kind of democracy we live in.*

Gutfeld, Greg. The Joy of Hate: How to Triumph over Whiners in the Age of Phony Outrage. Crown Forum. 2012.

> *"Hilarious observations on the manufactured outrage of an oversensitive, wussified culture."*

Carolla, Adam. *President Me: The America That's in My Head.* Dey Street Books. 2015.

> *Anybody looking for a good laugh, Adam does a great job pointing out the insanity of popular culture. If you're fan of straight talk, and honest opinions, this a great book.*

Documentaries:

War Made Easy: How Presidents & Pundits Keep Spinning Us to Death (2007)

Century of Self (2002)

Can We Take a Joke (2015)

"But…Seriously" (1993)

Chapter 5

The Economy

"A bank is a place that will lend you money if you can prove that you don't need it" – Bob Hope

We are constantly being told that the economy has recovered and doing great. If you look at Wall Street that seems the case on the surface, the numbers keep going up. It's like a pinball game on crack, but there is a homeless guy sleeping under it. Once you dig in a bit, you'll notice it resembles a Picasso Painting. From a quick glance it looks great, but once you get close, you notice everything looks fucked up.

Back here in the real world, Main Street continues to be plundered. As a result we are experiencing the highest: student loan debts, credit card debt, amount of people on food stamps, flat wages, and levels of REAL unemployment or under employment. Jobs that once produced a middle class income are being sent overseas. All the while 62 sons of bitches own half the wealth in the world? We are told by our leaders the recovery is doing great? What recovery are they talking about? Is there a sunken ship being recovered we should know about? Many may say work harder or reinvent yourself to get ahead, it doesn't address the fucked out model of neoliberal economics which is parasitically extracting our wealth and numbed the host. The middle class is the engine of the economy, and it's fading. Recovery spoken about by our politicians and news media is a fabrication. What do these charts indicate?

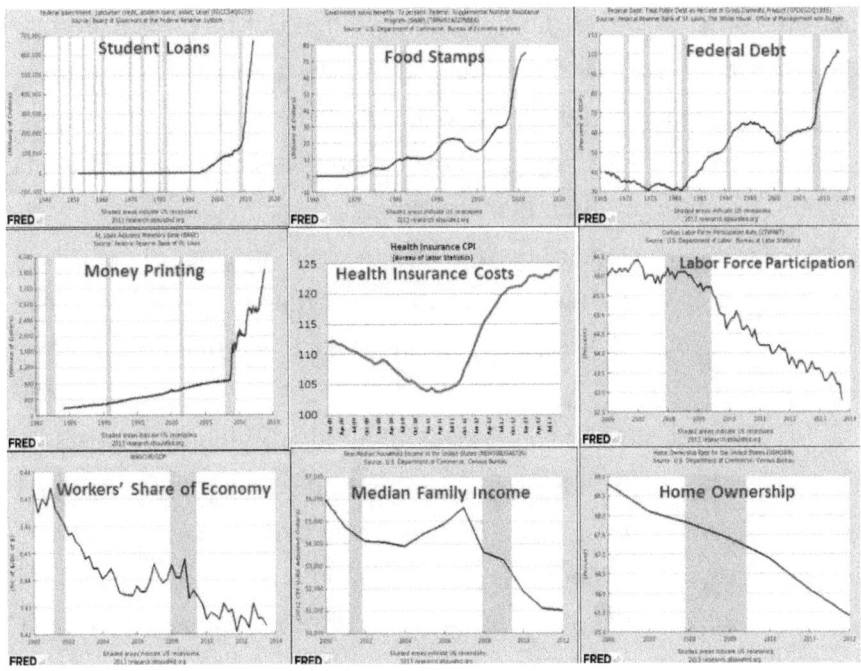

This is not capitalism, and neither is it socialism. The "Too Big to Fail" slogan was sold to the American public says it all folks. In capitalism there is no such thing as too big to fail. When business and government join forces "too big to fail" in reality is a fundamental hallmark of "fascism". The banking industry cannot fail because they financially control the government. People think fascism is being racist or having a thin mustache, which is false. That's just being a racist dick. It's the autocratic control of government and business.

We see this happening in real time with the Trans-Pacific Partnership trade agreement which are written in secret. It is another extension of the multinational take over. This numbing effect of neoliberal economics has rendered us with some kind of societal Stockholm syndrome where we are afraid to ask "what the hell is going on?" When we do, politicians ignore what we ask or shift focus to something else. Or they simply lie to our faces. We are being treated like a kid asking their mom where babies come from. You want a cookie Timmy or here play with the iPad? She isn't going to explain somebody got fucked, and neither do the politicians. Because like your mother, they are doing the fucking and don't want to talk about it. Instead of diving deep to get to the root of the problem, we are pointing our fingers at everything that moves. The idea of we need to regulate this, or that to fix this problem is not a solution.

There are no real solutions without identifying the genesis of the problems. It's like blaming door dings and a flat tire for the car not starting when the engine is blown up. We need to understand our monetary system upon which the economy is built is a giant turd. No matter what you say about it, amount of times you roll it in sugar, or spray frebreze on it; it came into this world as a steaming pile of shit, and it's still a piece of shit. Think about it, when big bankers working for the Fed or politicians are talking about the economy do you believe them? You don't, because they are full of shit. How often in real direct terms do they speak about the mechanics of the system? Answer: NEVER. They are not going to talk bad about a monetary system that doesn't work for us, but only works great for them. How many pimps turn themselves in for not treating their whores right? None, of course. It's ridiculous to think we're going to get a straight story from these people. When people to come out, and speak up those voices do not last in the oligarchy controlled media.

Now when we really think hard about money it is the only thing in this world that resembles real magic. It's willed into existence by people with power, it controls people but very few people understand it. Abracadabra money is willed into existence at the Fed by the issuance of debt. Bank bailouts? No problem, puff money into existence. Quantitative easing? No problem, puff money

112

into existence. Fractional reserve lending? No problem puff money into existence. It reminds me off the subprime auto lending. No job, no pulse, no arms to steer the car - no problem here's your car at 25% interest. All the while with every magical creation of money creates a counter spell of compounded interest which indebts those within its system in a layering effect debt servitude. All of this is heaped upon our backs while we are running on the economic treadmill going nowhere. In the old days money was attached to either gold or silver. People in the past were smarter than we give them credit, a stark reminder of the failure of our education system not passing down pertinent wisdom.

The purpose for binding currency to a rare commodity is because it held its value overtime and made it difficult to manipulate worth. Gold backed money in this sense is a lot like the idea of crypto currency like bit-coin, the amount is fixed. Granted newly found gold would add more supply to the system, but it was a pain in the ass to get. Real work was required, not a few key strokes from corrupt bankers that pop back and forth between top government regulation jobs and Wall Street. With money created at the whim of the Federal Reserve or through fractional reserve lending, savers are forced into the investment systems that seems to only profit a few and where your hard earned money is always at risk by those in control of the system. If great grandma Mildred put $4.11 under her mattress in 1913 and you found it in 2016 it would be worth $100 in today's buy power. Whereas when she hid that $100 in 1913 it was worth $2430 in today's currency.

"Paper money eventually returns to its intrinsic value -zero." - Voltaire

British economist John Maynard Keynes ideas have played a major impact on modern economic theory. His economic theories have been employed to further enrich and empower the people controlling the world financially. In 1944, he convened delegates in Bretton Woods, New Hampshire to negotiate the Bretton Woods system which gave birth to the IMF and World Bank. Keynes was a member of the Royal Institute for International Affairs a globalist think tank linked to the Council on Foreign Relations in the US. In his book, *The Economic Consequences of the Peace* published in 1919, he describes what we have been dealing with for the last century. This is the ground work of the austerity we are experiencing today. Where the elite keep getting richer by a made legal corrupt banking system, bailouts by the middleclass are used to pay for Wall Street mistakes, and no matter how much you tighten your belt it seems impossible to maintain financial security.

"Lenin is said to have declared that the best way to destroy the capitalist system was to debauch the currency. By a continuing process of inflation, governments can confiscate, secretly and unobserved, an important part of the wealth of their citizens. By this method they not only confiscate, but they confiscate arbitrarily; and, while the process impoverishes many, it actually enriches some. The sight of this arbitrary rearrangement of riches strikes not only at security, but at confidence in the equity of the existing distribution of wealth. Those to whom the system brings windfalls, beyond their deserts and even beyond their expectations or desires, become 'profiteers,' who are the object of the hatred of the bourgeoisie, whom the inflationism has impoverished, not less than of the proletariat. As the inflation proceeds and the real value of the currency fluctuates wildly from month to month, all permanent relations between debtors and creditors, which form the ultimate

*foundation of capitalism, become so utterly disordered as to be almost meaningless; and the process of wealth-getting degenerates into a gamble and a lottery. Lenin was certainly right. There is no subtler, no surer means of overturning the existing basis of society than to debauch the currency. The process engages all the hidden forces of economic law on the side of destruction, and does it in a manner which **not one man in a million is able to diagnose**." -John Maynard Keynes*

My general impression of Keynes is that he was a scholar commissioned to legitimize a convoluted and obfuscated system of economics that allows the elite money masters to carry on their compounding currency fraud that drains away all the rewards of our labor on war and other waste which equates to little benefit for us and an advancement of their goals. Then through the economic mechanisms of war and waste they are able to amplify their economic interest and power, thus being able to push society in a direction they desire. Instead of one in a million, **we need millions who can diagnose what is going on**. It is the only way we can stop this train of madness which is being directed without any concern for general welfare of humanity who is unknowingly riding coach getting drunk, eating cheese burgers, and watching movies. You don't need a fancy degree to figure this out, just eyes, ears, and a discerning mind. Keynes knew perfectly well the result of such a system would result in our present day conditions where 1% of the population own 40% of the wealth, and the bottom 80% percent has only 7% of the wealth.

Because of this ever inflating monetary system and the destruction of pensions it has created a necessity for people to put their money into the market to gain wealth. As Keynes describes within this system, "wealth-getting degenerates into a gamble and a lottery." As John Oliver explained on his show "Last Week Tonight", 401(k) fees are no laughing matter. Because of the complexity of these various investment schemes people are putting their money into investments they truly do not understand which makes it's ripe for fee gouging and getting screwed over. It takes a lot of work to become financially literate in such a complicated system, it's never taught to the general public. Most people working in the system only understand the portion applicable to their job. A lot of this money is poured into what is called "exotic investments". Much like "exotic women" it will likely leave you broken hearted with an empty bank account unless you are rich or speak her language of money.

When money was attached to a solid commodity that was a pain in the ass to get it was much more difficult to manipulate the value of currency and people's savings. For centuries alchemist dreamed of way to magically transform lead to gold. A way of creating money from nothing. Where the alchemists failed, the bankers succeeded when they were able establish the Federal Reserve and abolish the gold standard. Now the game is set with them able to simultaneously play banker and player with virtually a never ending supply of money. The ability to buy up real assets, real production, and real ideas out of nothing.

With some clicks of a mouse, and key strokes money is created. Money is made by computer algorithms exacting trades on the stock market in microseconds while a small portion of people profit greatly; all the while we are working our asses off just doesn't make sense. When the real money we all depend on and work for is in a system that resembles a game called Cookie Clicker (Google it). We should probably start asking a lot of questions and demanding change. The aim of the game is to bake cookies at as great of a rate as possible; as such, there is no true end to the gameplay. To start the game, the player bakes cookies solely by clicking on a giant cookie, gaining one cookie each time it is clicked. Cookies are used as currency to buy items like grandmas and farms that bake cookies without user input and upgrades that increase the number of cookies per click and unit time. The abstract nature of the cookie currency and real money in the computer is basically the same, however the real money is what you and I need to survive. Instead of buying virtual grandmas and farms, they are able to purchase real assets and make your grandma work at Walmart instead of making cookies for her grandchildren. How is it that people keep getting richer and richer without producing anything of value? We should be pissed off, people are playing cookie clicker with real money the rest of us have to work for it. It's reminiscent of Star Wars when Obi-Wan waved his hand and said, "Nothing to see here... move along... move along..." Money must be magic...

"I just don't trust any of it. Every time I read something about how there's been another ridiculous climb of the Down Jones, there's a part of me goes, "This can't be good". None of this is real money. You know what I mean? It's not like there's actually more of anything. It's just ideas. When people are getting richer and richer but they're not actually producing anything, it can't end well." -Louis C.K.

A real world example of cookie-clicker economics is General Electric. In the 1970's General Electric could make more profit by playing games with money than actually producing goods in the United States. General Electric is more of a finical institution than it is a producer. It makes over half its profits by cookie-clicker economics, moving 1's and 0's around than it does contributing to the real economy. Then add in the offshoring of jobs; we start to get

117

a picture why we are where we are at financially. Just to add insult to injury tax payers bailed them out in 2008 when their cookie-clicker economic games went belly up. Times this by a bunch of large multinational and finance companies and a crystal clear picture starts to emerge.

Money – Money - Money

We all think about money, we deal with it day in and day out. It is integral to our daily lives, but we do not fully realize all the backstage machination. It's been around for thousands of years and it makes trading commodities easier. It was easier to store value made out of gold or silver than it was bushels of wheat or dragging a goat around for barter. Money hasn't really ever had an intrinsic value, especially today with our fiat paper money. All it's really intrinsically good for is wiping your ass or maybe making a fire. It's merely a symbol of what you can purchase that has intrinsic value.

The symbolism of it goes a bit deeper, when you recognizance that it represents human energy or human life. It follows the same basic rules of electricity or other natural energy systems which is interesting. When you take time to think about it hard enough you'll would find that economics is a social extension of a natural energy system which incorporates humanity. Power is rate of doing work, it's your production value. The more you produce, the more you're rewarded right? In a moral economy sure, but in our parasitic system non-producing entities soak up the lion's share of the riches. When you work and get your pay check you're receiving a quantified amount of human power that represents your life. That is why people are said to be worth X amount of dollars, it can be taken a bit more literally than what we give it credit. Money is power due to the simple fact it represents the quantification of human life. The more of it you have, the more power and influence you can wield.

The power and influence of money is immense when you really think about it. The discussion of money is politics in the popular media is extremely limited. For good reason, the media is owned by the people who have all the money. If money can influence women who are 10's and reasonably intelligent to get with old ass wrinkly guys or complete nerds you better believe it controls politics. Think about it. If there is ever a societal system that should be kept free from fuckery it is the monetary system because of what it symbolizes, and how it effects our daily lives regardless of political party, race or religion.

"I believe that banking institutions are more dangerous to our liberties than standing armies. If the American people ever allow private banks to control the issue of their currency, first by inflation, then by deflation, the banks and corporations that will grow up around (the banks) will deprive the people of all property until their children wake-up homeless on the continent their fathers conquered. The issuing power should be taken from banks and restored to the people, to whom it properly belongs." -Thomas Jefferson

Our Monetary System

Most Americans do not understand in any meaningful way exactly how the financial sector runs. It has intentionally been constructed as a wandering, baffling maze of dead ends designed to keep the average citizen in the dark, forced to trust their elected officials, so called experts, and the media reinforces the lie by saying everything is ok. But everything is not ok. It's like the "big is beautiful" movement, but worse. Not matter how its spun being fat is never healthy.

As we take an honest dive into the function of our monetary system one thing will becomes clear quickly, we are getting ripped off. Regardless of whether or not we realize it, or want to realize it. We are playing a complex and convoluted game of monopoly with big brother. I'm sure you've all played monopoly with the kid who cheats, normally it's your older brother doing the cheating. Or maybe the shifty neighbor kid who lives down the street. He takes money out of the bank when nobody is looking, and buys up the board around you. Before long he has hotels on Boardwalk, owns all the utilities, while you are scraping by just to get around GO to collect your $200 dollars. Every space he lands on turns into a business opportunity for investment because he essentially has a never ending money supply.

In essence, this is why everyone is broke and why all the wealth is held in the hands of a small elite minority. The game is fundamentally rigged just like playing with your jerk older brother. A quick example of the rigging was during the 2008 crisis. Henry Paulson was the US Treasure Secretary. Prior to that he was the CEO of Goldman Sachs. He gets in front of the American people and says he's going to save us and we need to bail out the banks. See the conflict interest here? At US tax payers expense, he bailed himself and his fellow bankers out. They got to hold on to their enormous wealth, and power. With this kind of stellar judgment, it would be like a woman's advocacy group sending Bill Cosby with a giant bottle ruffies to a sorority's slumber party to judge a pillow fight, and having the girls pay for it. Either way, somebody is getting unknowingly screwed.

The social ramifications of this system have been manifesting themselves. As the economic prosperity is siphoned from the people there is pressure which causes societal cracks along race and ideological lines. It happened in Rome, it's happening now. Most

120

people feel something isn't right when they work their ass off, make a decent wage, and can never get ahead. When I was growing up my father worked as a mechanic and provided for a large family while my mother stayed at home. We lived modestly, but never went without. Now 30 years later as empty nesters, my father still works as a mechanic and my mother works part time. They still live modestly, but are no better off financially then they were 30 years ago with a house full of kids. They don't go into debt, or spend frivolously, but still eke out the same standard of living. This is the result of our monetary system which we as a people should be actively attacking its very existence.

The massive psychological hoodwinking behind this phenomenon is astounding. People are willing to accept economically on a whole everything is going to hell in hand basket, but unwilling to accept WHY it's that way. It's like accepting you have lung cancer, but deny smoking for 50 years played a role in its development.

If enough people truly understood our monetary system it would change the world overnight. We would be storming the castle with pitch forks and torches. In those days it wasn't hard to put two and two together and know exactly how you are getting fucked. You worked your ass off and the aristocracy would ride in and take a part of your harvest and goods. Today, it's basically the same story except the methods are less overt. Bankers and economist make it sound so complex that it's boarding on magic that most people give up, and move on with life. Let's go back in time and see how this monstrosity was built.

"It is well enough that people of the nation do not understand our banking and monetary system, for if they did, I believe there would be a revolution before tomorrow morning." -Henry Ford

121

The Federal Reserve

According to the Fed's website, "After Alexander Hamilton spearheaded a movement advocating the creation of a central bank, the first bank of the United States was established in 1791." Awesome right? No! This Bank went on for about 20 years, but people saw that it had too much influence. They actually understood money generation in those days, it was rejected and not renewed. Then just like a case of herpes, the bankers were back in 1816 to charter a second central bank and a bill was introduced to Congress. This bank was a lot like the first bank except bigger, and this bank also lasted about 20 years until people realized that this was a bad idea. Just maybe our founding fathers knew a thing or two when they were talking about central banks controlling monetary supply? In 1907, a severe financial panic jolted Wall Street. Many banks failed, and Americans thought the banking structure needed an overhaul. What needs to be understood, is that banks JP Morgan, and trust companies were competitors. Many allege Morgan used rumor and innuendo to create panic among the public which is very likely. Robert Owens, who "co-authored" the Federal Reserve act later testified before Congress that the banking industry had conspired to create a series of financial panics in order to rouse the people to demand "reforms" that served the interests of the financiers.

At the heart of most economic panics is speculation. It is certainly true in this case. People associated with running Knickbocker Trust were also engaged in using depositors' funds to corner the market in United Copper shares in an attempt to make huge profits. However, their manipulation fell on its face. When word got out what was going on panic spread and the Stock Exchange fell a staggering 48%. The Treasury Department stepped in with a $25 million deposit in New York banks. J.P. Morgan partnered up with John D. Rockefeller to organize a pool of money to shore up the markets and ease panic. Public confidence needed to be restored, and consequently the bankers talked to the press to persuade the public that the worst was over. These actions led to a return of stability on Wall Street, and some peace of mind among the public. The media also heaped praise upon JP Morgan and the powerful banking elite as the saviors of the crisis, even though bankers caused the problem in the first place.

Very important to note during this period of time, Morgan persuaded anti-trust busting President Roosevelt to allow U.S. Steel to acquire the Tennessee Coal, Iron and Railroad Company. By using this crisis Morgan was able to further consolidate his monopoly of the US steel industry by absorbing his largest competitor on the cheap as the market had bottomed out. The head of U.S. Steel and a high representative of Morgan met privately with President Roosevelt. They told him to control the panic U.S. Steel needed acquire Tennessee Coal and Iron. Roosevelt agreed, and the deal went through. With this backroom deal, they side stepped the Sherman Act which outlawed monopolistic business practices. It was an unstated, and unwritten political deal between the nation's most powerful politicians and bankers. This collusion is still alive and well today. In fact, it's more rapid if you look at the insane about of money spent on lobbing and the "think-tank" groups which consist of the business and political elite such as the Trilateral Commission and the Council on Foreign Relations (CFR).

In 1913, there was another push for a central bank called the Glass-Owen Bill. It was signed into law by Woodrow Wilson. A couple of words about Woodrow. In some circles he is regarded as the worst president. I'd have to agree, he was a sack of shit. He was a patsy of the bankers. He met with a wealthy banker Bernard Baruch (CFR) multiple times, and received political support to pass central banking legislation. Baruch was chairman of the War Industries Board, and under his leadership mobilized the US into the First World War Wilson. He was also advised by the "kingmaker" Edward House (CFR) who was backed and supported by Rockefeller's National City Bank. Politicians being bought off by bankers is nothing new. Before the elite had a strangle hold on the media, it was a popular news topic. So how was this Federal Reserve Act created? Was it drafted in congress? Nope. Was it drafted in secret? Yes.

The plan for the establishment of the Federal Reserve was carried out on an island off the coast of Georgia, Jekyll Island, in 1910. This bill was drafted under great secrecy. Normally when plans are made in secret, away from public view, it's usually never a good thing unless it's a surprise party. Jekyll Island was a vacation destination for the super-rich like the Rockefeller's or JP Morgan. Senator Nelson Aldrich, the Republican whip in the Senate and the chair of the National Monetary Commission sent his private railroad car to the New Jersey railroad station where he and five others met. Back in the early 1900's private railroad cars were like today's private jets. The interiors looked like rolling palaces. Abraham Lincoln disliked them so much he never rode in the car supplied for his service as president expect for when he was in his coffin. The members of the party were instructed to arrive separately and act like they didn't know each other. Aldrich who wrote the original bill a decade earlier which was turned down was the organizer. He was a business associate of JP Morgan and the father in law to John D Rockefeller. It doesn't take a genius to see where his loyalties lied. Absolutely no conflict of interest there right? So who was else was in this motley crew?

Nelson Aldrich invited Abram Piatt Andrew Jr. assistant secretary of the Treasury. Frank Vanderlip was there representing William Rockefeller. Henry Davidson and Benjamin Strong representing JP Morgan. Lastly, Paul Warburg was a partner at Kuhn Loeb and company who was representing the Rothchild interests. These guys who had been competitors decided to join forces so they could form a banking cartel and wouldn't have to compete with each other. Rich and powerful men meeting together to create a system to control the numerical representation of human energy should make a thinking person a bit nervous. Think of all the altruistic rich and powerful people in history? Not many, right. For over a week these men met ironing out a plan which eventually became the Federal Reserve. This cartel went into partnership with the government. They had five objectives they were trying to achieve.

1. They wanted to stop the competition of other growing banks.
2. They wanted the ability to create money out of nothing for the purpose of lending.
3. To gain control of all the banks reserves of the reckless banks so they wouldn't be exposed to currency drains and or bank runs.
4. Shift loses from the bank owners to the taxpayers.
5. To convince the congress that the purpose of this bill was to protect the public.

After Woodrow Wilson signed the Federal Reserve into law. The Fed started with no money just a check book. The government could go directly to the Fed for instant cash without having to consult us pesky taxpayers all the while we are on the hook. Just look at the ridiculous national debt calculator. Quite the concept, money created out of nothing given to the government which we have to pay back plus interest to the banks.

The Fed is not much different than OPEC, however instead of oil it's a money cartel. A money cartel which formed a hybrid corporate-government partnership for the monopoly of producing currency. This organization and its member banks operate under the protection of the federal government while reaping vast profits. There are no elected officials at the Federal Reserve. The people who are in change seem to go in and out of public service at top banking positions.

Hmmm, could these people possibly have huge conflicts of interest? Would these people make decisions that would be good for the common people at the cost of their owners or fellow cronies? Yeah, not likely if history is any indication. Take the 2008 bailouts for example, which provided a huge transfer of wealth from the middle up to the richest should be a resounding NO. They don't care about us. We are nothing more than beast of burden in this system. In other words, we are the energy that propels it, but we reap little of the benefits.

After the bailouts, Banks had some of highest profits. That surely didn't trickle down to the rest of us. Consider how well they were rewarded for doing a shitty job and all their golden parachutes. The Fed is not owned by the government. It's owned by its private member banks. It owes their existence to the passage of an unconstitutional act by congress. Claiming it's the people's bank or for our good is complete bullshit. If it was, employees of the Fed would be government employees which they are not. There have only been a few politicians who have taken on the Federal Reserve: John F. Kennedy, Ron Paul, and few others.

"The modern banking system manufactures money out of nothing. The process is perhaps the most astounding piece of sleight of hand that was ever invented. Banking was conceived in iniquity and born in sin. **Bankers own the earth. Take it away from them, but leave them the power to create money and control credit, and with the flick of a pen, they will create enough money to buy it back again. Take this great power away from the bankers and all the great fortunes like mine will disappear, and they ought to disappear, for this would be a better and happier world to live in.** *But if you want to continue the slaves of bankers and pay the cost of your own slavery, let them continue to create money and to control credit." - Sir Josiah Stamp, Director and President of the Bank of England during the 1920's.*

The establishment of this monetary system made possible the development of the ideology of neoliberal economics over the past few decades. It's the driving economic philosophy which guided our past to this point, but few truly understand it. This ideology produced such gems as: trickle-down economics, free trade (export jobs/create trade deficits), destruction of main street, and the raise of huge multinationals which have more wealth that most nations. This neoliberal economic ideology does not work, its believers are like cult members. It seems to benefits the ones in charge, but everyone is getting screwed and they keep believing in the nonsense anyway.

"Trickle-down economics -- it didn't work. The whole idea was supply-side economics: give rich people a lot of money; they'll spend it, it'll go into the economy. Here's what we found out -- rich people, really good at keeping all the money. That's how they got rich. If you want it in the economy, give it to the poor people. You know what they're really good at? Spending all their money." -Greg Fitzsimmons

The function of money in an economy on the macro level functions a lot like water, and why wouldn't it? Both are systems which promote subsistence and growth. When you ponder about it in those terms, its function is common sense regardless of how confusing people make it sound or the ideology attached to it. This fact is further bolstered by the term coined as "trickle-down economics". The global economy is suffering because there is too much central bank money printing going into too few hands.

It's analogous to having an out of control flood with most of the money being dammed up, and not irrigated through channels which promote growth and the wellbeing to everyone else. This money is being held up in the financial market dam and not being let into farmland for doing productive things like growing crops or turning turbines to produce electricity.

We see the results in the form of record high stock market numbers, low real economic growth, and record high levels of consumer debt. This money just sits there and stagnates in concentrated pools of Wall Street wealth. As a result, general public is becoming more and more economically and politically discontent. Since they are holding all this water, they continue to give a little water to the politicians to change rules which will help reinforce their dam. This further chokes off the supply to the real economy. Hmmm… On the macro-level, can we draw a line of causality from record high profits in the financial industry to record high wealth inequality to highest indebted population? Yes, the line is very clear. It's not complicated, if you cut through the bullshit.

The question is: are the people in charge such as Alan Greenspan, Janet Yellen, Ben Bernanke and etc. stupid or economic psychopaths only looking out for the best interest of their cronies? The dam is starting to break under its own stress, because money isn't getting to where it needs to go. This is called the Velocity of Money, basically it's the rate of money switching hands. Currently, the supply of money slushing around in financial markets is at an all-time high, while the Velocity of Money is at all-time low. Common Sense conclusion, a ridiculously small amount of money is trickling down while a very small group of super elite continue to get richer. In the trickle-down economics scheme, our economy is an 80 year old man with an enlarge prostate and a case of kidney stones who needs to take a piss.

Neoliberalism Economics

The problem with Neoliberalism is that most people don't know what it is, and they are effected by its ideology day in and day out. It's a lot like HPV in that regard. It goes by many names: genital warts, free trade, condyloma acuminatum, capitalism, fig wart, etc. It wasn't until recently did we fully understand how bad HPV was and that it led to worse things like cancer. Much like HPV, we are finding out the ideology of neoliberalism is a sickness worse than first thought. What needs to be understood, there is a difference between classical capitalism championed by Adam Smith and what we are calling capitalism. Smith railed against monopolies and political influence which accompanies out of control economic power.

Capitalism is a lot like Miley Cyrus, started off great and with good morals. Something you wouldn't mind your kids growing up with. Then over time, people wanted to exploit her to make more money making her undergo a transformation which is analogous to neoliberalism. Our economy has handlers and so does she. Now she's riding a wrecking ball resembling the threat of destruction of our economic system.

We have a tightly knit financial network of monopoly which controls most of the world's wealth and influence. The results of this economic ideology is being manifest in: people hiding money offshore, loss of domestic manufacturing, stagnant pay of the middle class, and an emergence of race tensions in under privileged groups. This ideology is squeezing society, and those with the least are starting to lash out in various ways out of desperation. However, as a society we are responding to these economic and societal issues as if they are isolated. We should be thinking that maybe this screwed up ideology of economics is catalyst of these problems. This is not free market capitalism. This is an economic ideology which has resulted in a financial monopoly in control of the world's wealth.

In the days of feudalism when the peasants where being taken advantage of by their overloads they would rise up in rebellion and storm the castle with pitchforks and torches. The economic system was simple, they rode in on horses and took your shit. Now the people on horseback have taken form of a crazy difficult to understand monetary creation system, compounded interest, complex taxes codes, and an ideology that doesn't make any rational sense. I'm sure our system would look completely different if we got paid cash and someone rode in, swiped a huge chunk of it, and rode off instead of complicated system we are forced to live in and sustain. Feudalism has returned, and an oligarchy has been created. How much worse do things have to get before we collectively sharpen our pitch forks and light our torches?

One of the first things to understand about Neoliberalism is that it supposes that the economic actors are rational, and the market should self-adjust in a rational sense. The first folly in this supposition is to figure that the actors are rational and not fueled by greed. The second folly is to suppose that institutional greed isn't going to take over rational sense when it comes to regulation of the system where gaming the system is the ultimate goal in creating vast wealth. The self-profiting operators of this system are influencing the rules should be trusted as much as an unattended class of 6 year olds in candy store. There is going to be a rush on the candy, followed by a candy high, and finally a crash. It seems most neoliberal economist are only looking at numbers without truly taking in the big picture, and considering psychological implication of the consumerist propaganda which celebrates greed. A critical part of true economics is understanding how people think, the history of money, and what money really represents in human terms. Without a context of history and sociology, economics becomes meaningless and you are doomed to repeat past mistakes.

Regardless of the party, left or right, it seems both sides have bought into this thought disease. In fact, this ideology only benefits the super-rich who pay for soulless creatures called politicians to get into office. In the 1980 when Ronald Reagan and Margaret Thatcher took the ball of Neoliberalism and ran with it. Massive tax cuts for the rich, union busting, deregulation, privatization, and outsourcing the manufacturing base of developed countries followed. Companies now had the ability to operate free from trade unions and collective bargaining agreements which resulted in suppressed wages and benefits. It turns out the freedom of neoliberalism is only granted to the super rich and large corporations resulting in further exploitation of middle and lower classes of society. Before neoliberalism went into full swing, families could afford for a parent to stay at home and raise the kids, had only a house payment, and student loan debt was unheard of.

The rest of the world got this system force fed to them by the IMF, World Bank, and the World Trade Organization as economic "aid" in the form of loans that citizens of these poor countries are on the hook to payback. This "aid" money is then partially embezzled by the rulers, contracts given to large multinationals companies to do the work who are owned in large part by the financial sector. Meanwhile, the poor citizen are on the hook to pay back the money. Also, included with the "aid" are strings which dictate economic rules which negatively affects the people of those nations. Not much different than the subprime market targeting minorities in the early 2000's just executed on a world level. Economic Freedom was the battle cry, but the result was economic servitude. We should really be questioning why is Africa so poor when it is so resource rich?

We like to believe it's just because they can't get their shit together. However, it is hard to get your shit together when foreign countries and economic interests are constantly toppling governments and causing war. Libya is a perfect example of this phenomenon. Yes, Gadhafi was a weirdo dictator, but he gave his people free education, housing, and the highest standard of living in Africa. How did he do this? He nationalized the natural resources and the people benefitted rather than large multinational corporations taking the natural resources. Before the US and NATO got involved it was one of the most liberal countries in the Middle East. Women had rights, education was valued, and real progress was being made. In fact, it was a much better than place than Saudi Arabia where they average a beheading every other day and lash people for tweets they don't like. Why are we friends with Saudi? The real question should be asked who's economically or politically benefiting from our friendship with Saudi Arabia? By any real measure they are much bigger assholes than Gadhafi ever was.

Another symptom of this ideology is the privatization of public services. Water, energy, healthcare, roads, and prisons have been privatized at various places around the world. Sure people may say that it's good it can get done cheaper, but at what cost to society. Especially if you consider the control of those essential services are

132

held in trust by the same people who control the monetary system. Do you really want powerful corporations owning the water you drink, your healthcare, and energy we use? If they are paying for the politicians, just who are they responsible to? Nobody, but themselves. World Bank has been pushing this for years. By going down this road of privatization, the people own less and the corporations and the elite own more. They have you over a barrel, they control and own everything. When services we all use are owned my financial power brokers, profit motive is priority, and people are squeezed. In turn, less money goes back into the real economy, and more goes to the top. These people in control who want to own everything do not think even water is a basic public right. At least that is what Chairman, Peter Brabeck-Lethmathe, of Nestle thinks. There has been a movement underway for major financial players to buy up water right. Even the Bush family has gotten into the water buying game purchasing 300,000 acers of water reserves in Paraguay.

There is a guy from Nestle doesn't think water is a human right… This guy wants to own the rain. Can we do something about this guy? You work at Nestle, you're supposed to be happy and making cocoa for people. This guy is like well people are running out of water. What if we owned all the water and kept it under our place in the future when everybody's. That's why I a picture the guy talking, "I want to own all the water. I want to have it underneath my house. And come to the door in a robe slightly ajar." He's a complete animal. –Bill Burr

How have we personally dealt with Neoliberalism? Most people have turned to debt. Notice in most cases two wages earners are needed to support a household. Currently, we are the most indebted people in history. Sure, part of it at the fault of the individual, however the architecture of this system plays a critical role. The interest we pay is essentially unearned income that accrues without any effort by the banks on money created out of thin air. When most people think about paying interest, the picture of lending their own money that they have earned is what's in most people's minds. They expect a return because of the opportunity cost of not having access to the money. However, that interest you are paying is on money magically created through fractional reserve lending at the bank. They are lending you money they created out of thin air. Come over and I'll give you some money I copied off my ink jet printer so you can buy a house. Now I want you to work for 30 years paying me back money, the money I printed with my ink jet. I'd go to prison for this, bankers get rich.

The problem with these policies pushed by Reagan, Clinton, Bush, and Obama is that they are prone to market failures. Too big to fail comes to mind. So what happens with these huge corporations become so powerful they are presumed too big to fail? The tax payer via the federal government has to bail them out. According to former Italian dictator, Benito Mussolini, "Fascism should more appropriate be called Corporatism because it is a merger of state and corporate power." Competition cannot run its course if they are not allowed to fail. As this system fails, we see how there is a retrenchment in tax cuts, and further deregulation for only the largest interests.

Deregulation is the battle cry you hear to fix the problems. However, what does that mean? Regulations come in all shapes and sizes. Some big and some small. Some good and some bad. Within this system, the small and middle size companies have been regulated out of existence making an eco-system friendly for the multinational companies to grow into all areas of life. Think about it. The food you eat, cars you drive, media you mentally consume, books your children learn from, the house you live in, and pretty much everything else you use to sustain your life is owned or supplied by large multinational corporations which stock holding go back to a relatively small number of tightly knit banking/financial institutions. Massive companies can afford to pay people to cut through all the red tape.

Large companies have been very successful in pushing deregulation when it comes to financing and trade. A perfect example is NFTA which was signed by Bill Clinton. Over a million US based manufacturing jobs have been lost. Due to this deregulation of trade, Mexico has 10 fairly new auto manufacturing plants. All the while, Detroit which was the capital of auto manufacturing has record high unemployment and crime. That whole areas of this country have been sacrificed for cheap labor and higher profits for stockholders of these multinational companies by a swipe of Clinton's pin. Sure, it made the companies more money. Sure the car could cost a little less now, but at what domestic financial and societal expense? Trimming costs are great, but this is like eating a tape worm to trim down. Fuck be the consequences. Other examples abound as the manufacturing base of this country has been systematically gutted on the road to a consumer only country. All of this is done to further enrich the elite of the country, and push financial domination globally.

In 1999 our buddy Bill Clinton signed the repeal of the Glass-Steagall law which separated commercial and investment banking. This regulation was put into law in 1933 due the Great Depression. Banks would be allowed to take deposits and make loans. Brokers would be allowed to underwrite and sell securities. No firm could do both because of the conflict of interest. In other words, banks making loans had to hold onto them and could not sell them on the open market. This protected the depositor from speculation.

This deregulation of the financial markets made it possible to write shitty loans and make a ton of money in the short term by selling them on the secondary market as mortgage backed securities. This caused the housing bubble that peaked in 2007 which popped in 2008. Anyone with half a brain could see how this could be a conflict of interest. Selling mortgage backed securities in this manner is not unlike buying a used car from a shady Russian guy. He put the wrecked car back together with bubble gum and bailing wire and sold it for the bluebook price. It looks good, it has a defined book value, but in reality it's structurally and mechanically unsound and it isn't worth shit. Same with the mortgage backed securities, selling lemons. After the bailout, was regulation put back into place from stop this from happening? Common sense would say yes, but no. They made lending guidelines a bit stricter as a response. The same bullshit is still going on, and another bubble of epic proportions is growing again. It's encompassing much more than just the housing market, and only God knows what will happen when it pops.

It's like a 40 year old Vinnie who spends all his time at the track and still lives with his mother. He's always speculating and betting on the horses. By repealing, Glass-Steagall he now has access to his mom's checking account. When his Mom found out he blew through the money she had to put a 2nd mortgage on the house to bail him out. Then after all this, he still has access to her checking account and was never held accountable. But now he is supposed to behave himself. She should be pissed, and so should we!

The Big Screw

There are so many things we take for granted that need to be question. This system on a macro-level functions to basically enslave everyone in debt bondage. It is nothing more than a form of legalized theft, and debt servitude. If you see how the system works, and apply words with their definitions, you get to see how horrible this is. People have a hard time with words and definitions these days. Instead of understanding what a defined term means, people want to change the definitions of words to make themselves emotionally feel better or run away from reality. I think our Prussian education system is largely at fault for this mess of stupidity, and the horrible command of language. Most people's heads explode when they figure this out because it's so messed up or they shove their head deeper into the sand. This monetary system and income tax all got started in 1913. Anyway, words to know. Let the definitions sink in.

Pledge - a thing that is given as security for the fulfillment of a contract or the payment of a debt and is liable to forfeiture in the event of failure.

Debt bondage - (also known as debt slavery or bonded labor) is a person's pledge of their labor or services as security for the repayment for a debt or other obligation. The services required to repay the debt may be undefined, and the services' duration may be undefined. Debt bondage can be passed on from generation to generation.

Forfeiture - the loss or giving up of something as a penalty for wrongdoing.

137

1. When you are born you are given a social security number. You are therefore **pledged** at birth. You are now **bonded labor**, on the hook for the national debt you personally had no hand in creating. In a very real sense everyone is born into financial bondage because of the national debt and our bank owned monetary system. Since you are largely made from carbon, think of yourself as a commodity of carbon that does work. Human collateral.

2. When money is created by the issuance of **bonds** we are the security (**bonded labor**). For the love of God, the word bond should be an indication we are getting fucked. It's right there in plain sight. There is a payment due every month on the principle plus the interest on every dollar in existence. It is a paradoxical impossibility to pay back this debt because its generation requires currency which has attached interest. **Perpetual debt bondage** is a result of such a paradoxical system. News flash, money doesn't have to be created in this manner which make us debt slaves.

3. The banks make money from selling the **bonds** (our **bonded labor**) and from the subsequent compounded interest. Much of our **bonded labor is owned** by large financial institutions and foreign governments. The common folks have some too, but the percentage is extremely small in comparison.

4. Throughout your life you spend a great deal of your time paying interest on that public debt which has been created to empower the people in control. They are receiving great sums off this generated debt.

138

5. A good deal of our **bonded labor** interest money goes to businesses which are owned or control by the same small group of inter-tangled financial interests which control most of the world's wealth. It's not hard to do when you've convinced everyone via this mechanism to unknowingly work for you for the last 100 years.

6. Now the banks we deal with day in and day out for financing our educations, putting a roof over our heads, and etc. are creating money from thin air by the means of fractional reserve lending. Which means when you deposit your money, they only need to hold on to 10% of it or less, and the rest of it they can use to invest in Wall Street to do whatever. From that 10%, they are able to lend out 90% more than what they have in possession and create new currency by the issuance of new loans. Then we pay them interest on the money they just created from thin air. This method creates the next layer of **debt bondage**.

7. By the means of the Wall Street boom and bust cycles they are able to cash in low on companies and industries that actually produce real goods and services amassing more control of the economic system. This process of boom and bust is nothing more than a transfer of wealth to the banking elites caused by the same people who caused the crashes to begin with. Think of it as harvesting after all the hard work has been done.

8. With this already insane system we need to add in inflation to screw normal working people. Our currency is subject to inflation due to its fiat nature. This erodes the wealth of

normal people who are "savers". Notice how prices of things like food, healthcare, etc. keep going up while your pay stagnates? Buying power of money tucked away in savings diminishes. For example, $5 dollars in 1988 is worth $10 dollars today.

9. Everything you buy has "hidden taxes" built into the price. Every step along the supply chain a good being produced has taxes built into it. We generally don't think about. I good portion of what you are paying for in an item has this built in tax due to this debt bondage system. Coming and going we are getting shook down by our economic bullies, there's no alternative route to get home from school.

10. Our reward? These extremely rich and powerful group of people control which laws get passed, and who's in office. They are in control of both political parties, government, media, medicine, food, and etc. They've made it possible for themselves to side step a lot of this system we get beat over the head with when they form their tax exempt philanthropic organizations, and other various loop holes to further their agenda.

11. If you don't want to take part in this criminal enterprise set up by the banksters. You have two options: 1) Live homeless like an **animal**. 2) Don't pay, and their government agent the IRS will lock you up like an **animal** as **forfeiture** to a **pledge** you never made except for being born. Either way, you are being treated as an animal. George Carlin was very literal when he said, "you have owners."

"Give a man a gun we can rob a bank. Give a man a bank he can rob the world." - Anonymous

This is not FREEDOM. This is a system of bondage and soft-slavery. There's no denying it unless we want to ignore portions of reality or change the meanings of words. When will we wake up to the fact that all men are free? We have been lead into a system where we have been yoked, and ignorantly praising the exploits of our unrecognized masters. How much worse and crazier does it have to get until we turn on our oppressors. This empire has reached its peak, it can either go two ways 1) transform into society that praises the higher ideals of being human or 2) it will crumb into chaos. The chaos is already starting to happen.

This is a threat to our wellbeing that far exceeds terrorism, undocumented works, or some BS war on drugs. We are born into debt servitude. The differences in religion, race, and sexual orientation are simply a distraction to keep up this scam. They don't want us united. If we did unit, we would be able to zero in on the real problems. The ramifications of this fucked up system are almost too much to comprehend when we start to figure in the lost opportunity costs, and how it's been used to push global dominance.

Many don't want to accept it as reality, and will try to argue against what is going on with bad arguments, and not looking at the whole picture. Start opening your minds and researching. Nothing will get better until this system is thrown in the trash bin of horrible ideas. It was created by power hungry greedy assholes to exploit the public for their economic and political gains. Any arguments to the contrary is horseshit. Look at what it is, how it works, and our current condition. You can explain and talk all day convincing some people that a clock is not a clock. However, no matter how much talking is done or who is convinced of what. The clock still exists.

141

The mechanism of its functioning working parts are still there, and turning. It performs a task regardless of how badly people do not want to tell time. It does what it's designed to do no matter what people say about it, so too with the Federal Reserve and our monetary system. Look past the bullshit, and see what is.

"Forget the politicians. The politicians are put there to give you the idea that you have freedom of choice. You don't. You have no choice. You have owners. They own you. They own everything. They own all the important land. They own and control the corporations. They've long since bought and paid for the Senate, the Congress, the state houses, the city halls. They got the judges in their back pockets and they own all the big media companies, so they control just about all of the news and information you get to hear. They got you by the balls. They spend billions of dollars every year lobbying. Lobbying to get what they want." -George Carlin

Money Masters

It's always interesting to hear what the masters of this rigged system are saying. All indicators point to it hitting the skids soon. Talking heads on the mainstream media talking about the day to day insight in Wall Street don't know anything. If you ever want the truth of any topic you always look to the real powerbrokers or policy writers. See what they are saying, and look at the economic indicators and see if there is consistency. Weigh out what is being said, and what you see with your rational mind.

Carl Icahn

He is a self-made billionaire worth over $17 billion dollars. He started as a stockbroker in the early 1960 and later formed his company Icahn & Co and later got into the business of taking controlling position in individual companies. Most of these companies are well known: Nabisco, TWA, Texaco, Phillips Petroleum, Western Union, Gulf & Western, Marvel Comics, Fairmont Hotels, Netflix, and the list goes on. He has ridden the wave of ups and downs and has made a fortune successfully navigating the waters. This is what Carl has to say about our current condition.

"One of the things that's causing it to fall is happening right under your nose, that we have no capital spending. Capital spending is going way down. In a society like us, manufacturing is important. I don't care, sooner or later, you can't just keep tweeting to each other. You can't text each other. We say we're a service economy, that's great, we're a service economy. What does that mean? That we text more to each other. Sooner or later, everyone is going to send a text to each other and say isn't that wonderful, so why should anybody work? Just sit there and text to each other or watch TV. So I am saying to you, this is what is happening as we speak. Capital spending is down, obviously. The last two years, I mean, it's just down four percent in the last quarter which is unheard of when you don't have a recession. Productivity has not grown. In fact, it's the lowest growing it's ever been as far growth goes. These are very important things in a capitalistic systems..." –Carl Icahn

"You see the GDP is not going up, I could give you a lot of reasons. But the most important is that the middle class worker is really, does

143

not have good jobs. This unemployment numbers are not accurate in one way, that a lot of these guys have left the work force, and two, these jobs aren't jobs aren't paying that well. So I'm saying that the middle class - that is why you saw the uprising for Bernie Sanders and you see it for Trump and you see Brexit and you see what's going on in Italy. I think there's an undercurrent of great unrest in our global economies. This "one percent", people resent it, and they resent government for allowing it to happen." –Carl Ichan

George Soros

Viewed by many as philanthropist, and by others as the "Real Dr. Evil". One thing is certain. He understands money and is part of the establishment. He knows the role it plays in the world, and has been a social engineer for decades with his immense wealth. He is known as "The Man Who Broke the Bank of England" because of historic short sale of $10 billion worth of pounds, making him a profit of $1 billion during the 1992 Black Wednesday UK currency crisis. His hedge fund firm has gained about 20 percent a year on average, and is worth around $30 Billion. Back in 2007 made some bearish moves which resulted in him profiting in the 2008 debacle. Recently, he has been making some moves and has been sharing his observations. A number of occasions he has been speaking out about the geopolitical climate in Europe which is concerning to the world economy. In mid-2016 he shorted stock (bet against the S&P 500) and bought gold and gold mining stocks. Investors view gold as potential safe haven during market collapse or recession. Plus when the shit hits the fan, and when everyone is rushing to protect their wealth with gold he got in when it was still cheap.

Regardless of what you think of Soros, he understands Global Economics. He got it right in England in 1992, got it right in

2007, and now he sees the writing on the wall and has made drastic moves to protect his wealth and profit on what is coming.

Jacob Rothschild

Yes, a Rothschild had to be thrown into the mix. Not because they are at the center of every conspiracy theory or because he has an uncanny resemblance to the rich and sinister Mr. Burns from the Simpson's. The reason he's important is because he and his family going back generations have been gaming the monetary system for their gain. Plus, they had their fingers in the pie when creating the Federal Reserve. Arguably this family has understood the connection between money, geopolitics, and sociology better than any in history.

"I care not what puppet is placed upon the throne of England to rule the Empire on which the sun never sets. The man who controls Britain's money supply controls the British Empire, and I control the money supply." -Nathan Mayer Rothschild

Generation after generation wealth, power, and knowledge has been passed down within this family. In 2016 this is what Jacob Rothschild had to say about the current economic conditions.

"The six month under review have seen central bankers continuing what is surely the greatest experiment in monetary policy in the history of the world. We are therefore in uncharted waters and it is impossible to predict the unintended consequences of very low interest rates, with some 30% of global government debt at negative yields, combined with quantitative easing on a massive scale. To date, at least in the stock market terms, the policy has been

145

successful with markets near their highs, while volatility on the whole has remained low. Nearly all classes of investment have been boosted by the rising tide. Meanwhile, growth remains anemic, with weak demand and deflation in many parts of the developed world." – Jacob Rothshild

In other worlds we are witnessing the outcome of neoliberal economics. Lots of money sloshing around in the stock market, but none of really doing anything productive hence the anemic growth. People have been brainwashed into thinking Wall Street numbers equal production when they have been in fact separated by the lunacy of this fiscal policy. He like Soros, have been making bearish moves to protect their money. Either way he'll be fine, he's mega rich. Imagine we are all on an airplane and the pilot is a descendant of one of the Wright brothers. For generations he and his family have been living and breathing aviation. Now he gets on the radio and tells the rest of us that what we are flying into something like nothing he's ever seen, and he starts taking maneuvers to protect himself. Here's the problem, he has an ejector seat with a golden parachute, and the rest of us are going down in the wreckage.

Alan Greenspan

Alan was the head of the Fed for close to 20 years. As a follower of the neoliberalism economic ideology he was ordained as some sort of economic Pope or Prophet. Like most false prophets he's full of shit supporting an ideology that screws people over. Most ideology pushers rarely question the tenants of their ideology until it's a bit too late. When asked by the House Committee if his ideology pushed him to make bad decisions, Greenspan said he found a "flaw" in his governing ideology that has led him to re-examine his thinking. Since the disaster of 2008 that his monetary policies created he's started to wise-up a bit and breakaway from his ideological thinking. Now in 2016, this failed prophet of monetary policy is giving new warnings because of what we are all observing without addressing the underlying causes.

"What the Fed does at this particular stage is less important than what the markets are doing. And what the markets are beginning to show us is acceleration in money supply for the first time in a very long time... We have a global problem of a shortage in productivity growth and it's not only the United States but it's pretty much around the world and it's being caused by the fact that the populations everywhere in the Western world, for example, are aging and we are not committing enough of our resources to fund that," –Alan Greenspan

He fails to mention that the Fed and its neoliberal economic ideology created this mess in the first place. They are giving out money dirt cheap to the financial sector. The financial sector takes that money and invests it in the stock market because its easy money, profits keep going up as the money supply keeps increasing. So why isn't money going into capital expenditures that go into the real economy? Because it's easier money to make money out of nothing on the stock market than to pay people to build machines, buildings, and make shit to get a return on investment. What direction is someone going to head if given the option to get paid $60K to tweet for a living or work their asses off to dig ditches? Of course they are going the route of least resistance. That is what is happening on a Macro level with our economy. Free Trade agreements like NFTA, and TPP which is being pushed on us by Obama are only going to make these problems worse because it eliminates domestic production with no real replacement. You cannot have productive growth without the ability to produce domestically. It's like a farmer bitching about his yield being low, but not taking into consideration he's been selling off his best land for years. It's insanity...

The hilarity continues when he ignores his role in creating the mess we've been dealing with and what is headed our way. This Priest of the Church of Neoliberal Economics, Alan Greenspan, does an about face, and says the solution to our problems is the gold standard. Ironically, he's starting to sound like Ron Paul.

"If we went back on the gold standard and we adhere to the actual structure of the gold standard as it existed prior to 1913, we'd be fine. Remember that the period 1870 to 1913 was one of the most aggressive periods economically that we've had in the United States, and that was a golden period of the gold standard. I'm known as a gold buy and everyone laughs at me, but why do central banks own gold now?" –Alan Greenspan

Anyone who has even a remedial education about the Federal Reserve knows that nearly all of America's economic woes can be directly tied to the fraudulent monetary system run by this money monopoly. Prior to 1913, the Federal Reserve did NOT EXIST. Ironic how he is calling for a monetary system that the Federal Reserve destroyed. Also, prior to 1913 Federal Income Tax did NOT EXIST. Go figure, when the Government creates money without issuance of debt on the heads of the citizens you are not taxed to the hilt to repay interest. In short, without realizing what he was saying he was advocating the end of the Fed to fix our economic problems.

Moving Forward?

After this monetary experiment goes down in a ball of flames, the automatic knee jerk reaction will be to a system that resembles socialism that is controlled by the top. That's the last thing we want to do is give the people who made the problems more power and authority. We are already seeing this movement with the popularity of Bernie Sanders running for democratic nomination. Bernie seems like a great guy, but taking care of people should be governed on a more local level not from on high like in Soviet Russia or by the Federal Government. The worst thing that could be done is to install more socialism into this quasi-cooperate fascist oligarchy we call the United States. There is no difference between what we call far left and far right. Fascism and Communism are fundamentally the same, a small amount of "elites" ruling over the rest via dictatorial view. The political spectrum of those being on each end is complete nonsense. There is being free vs. not being free. A perfect example of this has been Obamacare, and how that mandate made insurance premiums more costly. People should be rewarded for what they produce and accomplish that benefits society in fulfilling needs or wants. People shouldn't be rewarded for sitting around doing nothing productive, neither should people be paid extraordinary amounts for passing 1's and 0's around.

Since money represents something real for most people, hours of their life. It should be anchored in sound principles and reasoning. There are multiple options at our disposal. However, the system must be simple in design and regulation. If the system by nature is complicated only a small percentage of people within the system will understand it. Therefore, the system is open to exploitation. If the system is simple it will be less prone to exploitation because more people understand the rules. Its common sense in the microcosm when you are playing a board game, it's a lot harder to cheat if everyone knows and understands the rules. It should be a system taught to everyone in school thereby a reasonably educated person will understand the system which regulates the production of their society and their personal life. If a simplistic policy existed, transparency would exist and wasteful bureaucracy would be eliminated. Common people would have better control of their own futures rather than experts who are managing the quantified essence of their lives.

A free market system with simple regularity rules can exist which does not give power and money to banks and money managers to buy up the world, but keeps it in the hands of the common people and the real producers. Welfare systems can also exist in such a system. When the wealth is not being sucked into the financial mechanisms of the elite, and money isn't subject to parlor tricks - an equilibrium can exist which fosters wellbeing and security. Such systems have existed in the past, such as colonial script, but were pushed aside by those having interest in controlling the monetary supply and pushing their own political agendas. The question is, do we want a much more simple system of commerce that fairly rewards people efforts and takes care of needy, or a system we've had for the last 100 years which has pitted us against each other where stepping on somebody's head is celebrated by taking advantage of people via complex financial schemes?

This shit does not have to be that complicated. Why is there a multiplicity of rules which nobody understands except for the people making money from not producing anything of worth? Within this current system, unnecessary financial growths are sucking up quantified human energy at an alarming rate and growing larger and larger. In a physiological system, we call these tumors or cancer.

The economy, same as the human body, functions as a natural system. Unnecessary growths which require energy serve no purpose other than to make the overall system sick. Think about what's of worth to us human beings which promotes our happiness: stress free relationships, shelter, goods, services, food, leisure, infrastructure, medicinal, and teaching the young well. What is not of worth: an out of control financial industry passing 1's and 0's around which has siphoned the energy away from those basic elements of human happiness to benefit of a few. As a result, our economy resembles the elephant man, all covered in tumors. When the next bubble bursts, are the thinkers of this country going to unite behind common sense and demand change, or let the insanity continue? Please be a thinker.

"We spend money we don't have and blithely mortgage the future with a wink and a nod. Screw the next generation. It's about getting credit now, lookin' good for the upcoming election." -Confessions of Congressman X, anonymous Democratic congressman.

For the first time in history we have the ability to use the science of complex modeling to accurately model the function of complex systems and block-chain crypto-currency to decentralize our monetary system back into the hands of the people. It is possible to use such technology to level the playing field where those who produce are rewarded on merit, and a lending hand can be given people who need it. All we need to do is defy the banking powers and throw some nerds at the problem. If nerds figured out how to put a man on the moon, pushed the internet to lightning fast speeds to improve online porn, then they surely we can figure out an economic system that is fair using the science of complex modeling which is free from the mind disease of neoliberalism economics.

Every person should decide for themselves not to be willfully ignorant and understand the monetary system in they which live. Like it or not we are all swimming in the same cesspool, we should understand how it got that way. This understanding should be common monetary knowledge, not a scarcity to be exploited for the gain of a few. If such a system existed war would diminish, and peace would have a chance. Money being created out of nothing at the expense of the public debt wouldn't be an option for building empire. Here's a fact about empires, if you're not running it you're getting fucked, even if you think you are doing okay. Sooner or later you, your children, or your grandchildren are going to suffer. Empire is nothing more than a tower of social hierarchy engineered with fear of human suffering manipulated by money and power. The people on the top feel like Gods, those on the bottom are being ground to dust.

"The Upper Class keeps all the money pays none of the taxes. The Middle Class pays all of the taxes and does all the work. The Poor are there just to scare the shit out of the Middle Class. –George Carlin

Thinking Differently

To a large extent, we still live and think in terms of this largely 20th century economic reality created by the most rich and powerful 100 years ago in secrecy. As a result we are detached from the product of our labor as we toil within a system created to cheat us. We are disaffected by our lives on the corporate treadmill because we have no stake in its ownership while at the same time the middle class is losing ground. Due to technological advances and the institutionalization of almost every area of life we have become detached from our neighbors, our children, our communities, and even the land which harkens back to our natural way of being.

On some level we know something is wrong or missing from our lives. A void of real meaning and joy due to the mass produced consumer culture which has brainwashed us since birth. We are missing the connection with each other which promotes individualistic unity. Our economic system has created this divide and has separated us from our human nature. This way of being is in our DNA, we yearn for it even if we haven't yet actualized it. The idea of returning to that former way of life that allowed for an economy in which the work you performed or the creations you built gave you a sense of accomplishment. Not generated numbers in a crooked system where we buy things to feel the empty void. For generations we have been sold the idea the dissatisfaction of our modern cookie-cutter institutionalized top down dictated civilization is the human condition in and of itself. This is a lie. It is a cultural myth things have to be this way. We the people can decide otherwise. Can we see beyond the lies of our culture? I hope so.

"Those who are able to see beyond the shadows and lies of their culture will never be understood, let alone by the masses." - Plato

Human nature and what we value is coming to focus for more and more people. It is returning via the internet, people are able to create and sell their wares independent of the corporate system. The Industrial Era made the traditional craftsmen and artisans obsolete. It displaced famers from their farm lands. However, there is a return to the peer-to-peer systems of exchange. A huge movement for local organic farming is growing. Human nature expressed via the internet is creating new opportunities for workers to develop and market their own skills. It is also giving people the

153

freedom to live where they like. A pattern is emerging offering us a way for us to participate economically with people around us in more traditional sense via technology. It's bringing human interaction back home, among individuals, and not via big business and institutions.

The internet kicked up a lot of crazy, but in another sense has given us a new structure upon which to build a new type of society which harkens back to our human roots of dealing with each other directly. Why is this happening? In a deep sense we value each other, and we value freedom in a world which is trying to regulate and control us with ever increasing rules and regulations.

This building momentum can be seen in the popular developments of peer-to-peer based business such as: Airbnb, Esty, Podcasts, YouTube channels, and emergence of the open-source technology. Airbnb has become one of the largest accommodation companies as a result. It has given people an avenue to conduct commerce in a way before not possible. Why deal with and give money to an impersonal monolith when you can deal with real people just like you? Podcasts and YouTube channels are another important example. This has given people the opportunity to broadcast ideas without the filter of the mainstream media. Ideas can be presented and discussed in long format resulting in greater insight and intellectual understanding. People yearn for well-rounded conversations, this is the primary driver of the popularity of Podcasts. The reason this has been so successful is due to the virtual open market of the internet. The better ideas have been gravitated to, while the poor ideas fail. Information is shared freely, and in this open environment has sparked creativity and growth.

The missing component to the next step in human evolution is the freeing of the economic system controlled by the banking elite. Who's to say it might not be a bad idea of removing the ownership burden of the elite, and putting into the hands of the people who actually work for a company. Intrinsically, it makes more sense for people who work for a company to own it and profit, rather than some outside banking or financial firm who spun money out of nothing to buy it. If the workers were shareholders and elected/hired their board of directors, do you really think we would see jobs being sent overseas for more profit at the expense of our middle class economy? Of course not. Competition between companies would still exist. Motivation for personal improvement and progress would still be present. In fact, the company would probably value personal improvement more because of the mutually beneficial symbiotic relationship inherent in such a system between the business, the managers, and the shareholder employees. This is a closed loop system where feedback from various components (managers, employees, the business) govern the operation with the ultimate goal of cooperation to achieve productivity. Everyone has bought in a very real sense. To further drive home the point, cooperation and having some real skin in the game provides a real feeling of wellbeing. Brain chemicals Serotonin and Oxytocic which promote loyalty, trust, and belonging are released when we work in cooperation with each other. Imagine hearing good company news and actually having real ownership in the success, rather than just being a cog making profits for some faceless powerful company.

This kind of company is called Cooperatives. Mondragon, a company in Spain is one such example. In 2014, it employed over 74,117 people. They are united by a humanist concept of business, philosophy of participation and solidarity, and a shared business culture. The culture is rooted in a shared mission and a number of principles, corporate values and business policies. People get paid well, and have great benefits. The wage ratios do not exceed 9:1. Unlike what we see with some of biggest businesses were we experience ratios 500:1 up to 1000:1. At what point does that qualify as being a greedy dick, and we no longer tolerate such bullshit? Even J.P. Morgan said the ratio should be no larger than 20:1. One thing is working hard, being successful, and having some nice things. It's completely a different story, using a fucked up financial system to rob people and flaunt your money you legally stole. It's not hard to be rich in the financial sector when you can make your own money and can pay 5 lobbyist to 1 congressman to have laws passed in your favor.

There are already many reputable groups discussing this in academic circles. There are solutions which will benefit mankind much more than the existing system, and ideologies need to be laid down for this to happen. The solution must decentralize the power of central banking. There is no other way around it. It is the scourge of the earth. The Federal Reserve has to go. Of course this idea would not be popular in the political and banking circles because they are in bed with each other exploiting us. We don't owe them shit. Radical idea, but not if you think about it pragmatically.

Economic power should be in the people's hands who actually produce rather than a ruling banking class that doesn't do shit except for play with made up numbers which control our lives. We don't need a middleman who is robbing us blind. All money is a commodity of exchange for your labor and goods. Think about it. Materials to build a new house cost about as much as a nice car. The price of dirt costs are dependent on area of the country. Labor to build a new house is 1500-2000 hours. 2000 hours is what somebody spends working fulltime in a year. However, we spend 30 fucking years to pay off money magically created by the banks because we have to go through a middleman who is robbing us? In a practical sense this is nonsense. Something is definitely wrong with the system. By owning the means of exchange, we are owned by the system which is robbing our prosperity and freedom, and our children's futures. The first step is informing yourself and others of this horrible monetary system. The second step is demanding change.

If you want change it will only happen if you are informed.

There has been so much written and produced on the topic of our monetary policy. Below are some suggestions if you want more background on the troubles we are facing. The troubles will not go away until we recognize the problems and make them go away. Research what these authors are talking about. All of them have content independent of the books they have written, and can be looked up online. There are some great videos out there that should me watched.

Books:

Hudson, Michael. Killing the Host: How Financial Parasites and Debt Bondage the Global Economy. ISLET. 2015.

> *Professor of Economics Michael Hudson and former Wall Street analyst explains how economic policies were not just an honest mistake by desperate leaders trying to avoid the consequences of the wholesale looting of the US economy that began in earnest in the 1980s and culminated with the detonation of Warren Buffet's "financial weapons of mass destruction" in 2008. They were (and are) measures designed to keep in place the 'free lunch' enjoyed by a new money-based social order, one under which power and privilege are derived from the creation of yet more "debts that can't be repaid (and) won't be". The problem that will occupy the next few generations is how to undo the financial knots into which today's economies have been tied. Clearing away the overgrowth of debt requires countering the*

neoliberal junk economics crafted to disable society's defense mechanisms against financialization and unearned income.

Coogan, Gertrude Margaret. *Money Creators: Who Creates Money, Who Should Create It.* 1935

> *Coogan understood the difference between an honest money system and the unlawful debt money system in this country. She was a Security Analyst for The Northern Trust Company of Chicago. In her quest to uncover the root causes of monetary malfunction, she discovered facts that lead the way to simple, easy to implement solutions. She explains her findings about the monetary system without the obfuscating jargon. This is a refreshing contribution in a world of excess words without wisdom.*

O'Conner, Harvey. *Empire of Oil.* Monthly Review Press. 1955

Perkins, John. *Confessions of an Economic Hit Man.* Plume. *2005.*

Lundberg, Ferdinand. *America's 60 Families.* The Vanguard Press. 1937.

> *Between this book and "Empire of Oil", one can become quite disheartened about the political environment of the United States. Throw in "Confessions of an Economic Hit Man", and you'll have a trifecta of books proving to you that something is rotten and you are in the middle of it. The realization that a few rich people set the agenda for the world based on spreadsheets, land holdings, urban planning, labor relations, energy price manipulation and political favors and sponsorship. America's 60 Families takes you on an adventure of power manipulation and crooked lawmakers that our biggest movie producers can't describe. Get a good feel for why we needed Anti-Trust laws, and then swallow your red pill when you realize that the anti-monopoly rules only made it into law because another entity allowed them. Liberty? Free markets? Not on your life, pal. This was way back in 1938. With this background what is going on in the world becomes crystal clear.*

Griffin, G Edward. *The Creature from Jekyll Island: A Second Look at the Federal Reserve*. America Media. 2013.

> *Well researched work on the creation and effects of the Federal Reserve.*

John Maynard Keyes. *The Economic Consequences of the Peace*. 1919.

> *Obviously, an academic work. However, it shows how our monetary and economic policies have led to our current situation.*

Mark Blyth. *Austerity: The History of a Dangerous Idea*. Oxford University Press. May 2013

Documentaries or Videos:

Life Is Worth Losing – George Carlin (2005)

Revelations – Bill Hicks (1993)

Requiem for the American Dream. (2015)

America: Freedom to Fascism (2006)

Money for Nothing: Inside the Federal Reserve (2013)

Century of Enslavement: The History of the Federal Reserve (2014)

The Money Masters (1996)

Plutocracy: Political Repression in the USA (2015)

Four Horsemen (2013)

Overdose: The Next Financial Crisis (2012)

The Biggest Scam in the History of Mankind – Who Owns the Federal Reserve? (2013)

Chapter 6

Government

"You were born free, you got fucked out of half of it, and you wave a flag celebrating it." – Doug Stanhope

The liberty of the individual is under attack by the overreaching arm of the government and corporate interests. The elected public servant has been replaced by the oligarchic charlatan paying lips service to those they are supposed to represent. Instead of serving the good of the citizen they break public trust, and do the bidding of those who pay their way into office. The US is dominated by a rich and powerful elite. This is the exact reason why people are upset about money in politics and why nothing is getting better. The interests of the American public has no baring in the direction of the country or policy decisions. It doesn't take a rocket scientist to see that there seems to be an uneven playing field. The once level playing field that promoted wellbeing of America, and promoted the American Dream has been systematically disassembled.

"You came to this country or your great-grandparents came because it was an even playing field, and they were gonna sock away their money and maybe they didn't make it, but the next generation went to college and through perseverance and education made it." –
Adam Carolla

You can "Hope and Change" in one hand, and shit in the other - which is going to fill up faster? We have been walking around with a handful of shit for decades, and there is a reason for it. What we want is a level playing field, not handouts. A recent study by Princeton University noted. "Multivariate analysis indicates that economic elites and organized groups representing business interests have substantial independent impacts on US government policy, while average citizens and mass-based interest groups have little or no independent influence." In other words, the super-rich move policy while the average Americans have little power. With the force of their money, and an organized front these interest groups are able to run roughshod over the unorganized, infighting, and purposely misinformed public. This study concludes, "Americans do enjoy many features central to democratic governance, such as regular elections, freedom of speech and association and a widespread (if still contested) franchise. But we believe that if policymaking is dominated by powerful business organizations and a small number of affluent Americans, then America's claims to being a democratic society are seriously threatened." What does that mean? It means we live in feudalism controlled by an oligarchy if we want to call a spade a spade. Former President Jimmy Carter had this to say July 28, 2016 on the subject when interviewed by radio host and author Thom Hartmann.

"It violates the essence of what made America a great country in its political system. Now it's just an oligarchy with unlimited political bribery being the essence of getting the nominations for president or being elected president. And the same thing applies to governors, and U.S. Senators and congress members. So, now we've just seen a subversion of our political system as a payoff to major contributors, who want and expect, and sometimes get, favors for themselves after the election is over. ... At the present time the incumbents, Democrats and Republicans, look upon this unlimited money as a great benefit to themselves. Somebody that is already in Congress has a great deal more to sell." Jimmy Carter

In medieval Europe the nobility held lands given them from the Crown and the peasants worked for the support of overloads. This ruling class of government, royalty, and church dictated society by the control of information, ideology and currency. These were the days when they didn't want people literate, reading the Bible and thinking for themselves. The government had absolute power.

When you look around with an open mind do you think Adam Smith, the father of capitalism, was wrong when he wrote, "All for ourselves, and nothing for other people, seems, in every age of the world, to have been the vile maxim of the masters of mankind." The Declaration of Independence and the Constitution were written in an attempt to avoid such injustices, but these standards of freedom and liberty have been circumvented for personal greed and power. A sure sign the two party system is working for someone else is when Congress approval rating is at 11%. The only thing they seem to agree on are policies which further their power via globalization at the expense of the middle class.

"It is inaccurate to say I hate everything. I am strongly in favor of common sense, common honesty, and common decency. This makes me forever ineligible for public office." -H.L. Mencken, Journalist, Author, Societal Critic

Federal Government replaced the crown. The nobility was replaced by the bankers and owners of multinational corporations who own and control the real wealth and power. We have replaced the peasants. Just as in medieval times there are very few who really own anything, and everyone works for their masters in the form of interest and taxes. As our reward we get to enjoy more constrictive laws and regulations, secretive military industrial complex, the rise of a military police state that surveils us, and a "Pavlovian" education system that conditions us into being confused halfwits. As a result of this social engineering, more people have been disenfranchised resulting in the highest incarceration rates in the world.

We can't call ourselves land of the free when we have the most people caged like animals that is a perfect example of an oxymoron. Oxymoron is formed from two Greek words sharp and dull. You have to be pretty dull to see things are not going in a good direction. The value of family and community which is the heart and soul of society has been replaced by ever tightening monolithic federal mandates, laws, and soulless institutions. This is replacing the role of family and real community with institutions where they hold the levers of power. This is the breakdown of the civic virtue of western civilization. Western Culture is was built upon the premise that individual sovereignty is a right either bestowed by the creator or a quality inherent in all humans, NOT privileges granted by the state. What most do not understand is when quasi-cooperate-government power has taken possession of money, education, the media, and law making means your sovereignty and your rights are gone! Instead of people managing themselves on a local level, power has been usurped by an ever increasingly powerful central government making dictates.

"Sooner or later, the people in this country are gonna realize the government does not give a fuck about them! The government doesn't care about you, or your children, or your rights, or your welfare or your safety. It simply does not give a fuck about you! It's interested in its own power. That's the only thing. Keeping it and expanding it wherever possible." -George Carlin

The Power of Why?

In order to understand government we need to understand the people and their associations. We need to understand **why** regardless of the party which is in power nothing changes. We need to understand **why** regardless of the president and their promises they expand the federal powers. We need to understand **why** regardless of who's in charge they keep warring and killing people in foreign countries. We need to understand **why** the military industrial complex is so powerful. We need to understand **why** regardless of party in power trade agreements are created which is eroding our middle class. We need to understand **why** the government does not work for us, but we work for the government. We need to understand **why** the constitution no longer applies. We need to understand **why** the whole purpose of the constitution was to limit the power of government. We need to understand **why** the president who is supposed to be equal to congress has become a democratically elected term limited monarch. We need to understand **why** the president can call war without congressional approval. We need to understand **why** we need a fucking license to assemble to protest the government. How ironic, you need permission to show you're pissed. We need to understand **why** there has been a militarization of the police. We need to understand **why** the states have no rights except for what the federal government dictates. We need to understand **why** our news sucks, and the best investigative reporting on TV from a fucking comedian, John Oliver.

"None are more hopelessly enslaved than those who falsely believe they are free." –Johann Wolfgang von Goethe – philosopher, novelist, diplomat.

In order to understand **why** our country became an oligarchy, we need to understand **how** it got that way. In order to do that we need to identify: the players, follow their associations, the money, and finally accept facts. It's really not very complicated if we accept reality as it exist rather than wanting to bend reality to our desired perceptions. We are living in an oligarchy, controlled by a wealthy elite. First thing is first, we need to identity the association that has a guiding hand in US policy. This association is the Council on Foreign Relations and where it came from. Once you discover how this works, it all becomes crystal clear.

"The only difference between Obama and Bush is that Obama is killing more people. He's double the numbers now. Can you imagine if McCain had won and did precisely what Obama has done, with every speech and every political maneuver overseas? There'd be riots in the streets about people we're killing. And yet because it's Obama. and he's better looking and better at reading the teleprompter, we let him get away with it." -Penn Jellette

We're going in...

The main problem with broaching this topic of power and control is that there are a lot of people go from zero to crazy faster than a super car can get from zero to sixty. This subject has become more taboo than kissing cousins. Why is that? Are people afraid of reality, and what the voice of reason maybe telling them? Pointing out and discussing valid history, current events, and the players in a reasonable way is the aim here. There is plenty of well documented information out there to prove how we are getting fucked and by whom without destroying the argument by going to crazy town. Again, I'm not conspiracy theorist, I like to deal with factual reality. This is a discussion about historical data, present day observations, and you draw your own conclusions.

The term conspiracy has had all sorts of weird meanings and feelings attached to it which has resulted in people not exploring ideas. It's became a pejorative word, when in fact it's an expression of an idea that maybe some people are in cahoots doing some underhanded shit. It also has sidelined people who are going against the official narrative. The term "conspiracy theory" as a pejorative was started by the CIA to undermine questioning that was against the official narrative of the Kennedy assassination. However, if you ever read a history book what you'll be reading cover to cover are stories of conspiracy. Conspiracy is what moves history because good people throughout the ages seem to be afraid to face the fact their leaders are conniving dickheads. How naive to think we are living in the only time in human history free of conspiracy when the control of wealth, information, and governance is in the hands of a few with very little transparency. The natural byproduct of secrecy is conspiracy. We cannot and will not deny historical fact or logic because it makes us feel good. If you insist on a life in state of perpetual cognitive ease built upon false historical narratives, fairy tells, made up authority, all sustained by mental gymnastics built upon logical fallacies stop reading now and go join the Church of Scientology. What you want to feel is cognitive dissonance. That's your mind working in terms of logic destroying ideological thinking and uncovering inconvenient truths. Embrace it like a good burn at the gym. Feed that cognitive dissonance by learning more until understanding is achieved. Those feelings are the chains binding your mind being broken by reason. Only by confronting what causes cognitive dissonance do our minds open beyond the shadows and lies of our culture. Question everything. The words HOW and WHY are two very powerful tools in the English language and should be used more often. They are the crowbars of understanding which pry open the doors to understanding and leads from the worldview of descriptions to worldview of explanations.

"We were not born critical of existing society. There was a moment in our lives (or a month, or a year) when certain facts appeared before us, startled us, and then caused us to question beliefs that were strongly fixed in our consciousness – embedded there by years of family prejudices, orthodox schooling, imbibing of newspapers, radio, and television. This would seem to lead to a simple conclusion: that we all have an enormous responsibility to bring to

*the attention of others information they do not have, which has the
potential of causing them to rethink long-held ideas." –Howard Zinn
(Political Scientist and American Historian)*

Recognize when you put your head in the sand you are
giving the government permission to fuck you with its red, white,
and blue dick by the means of corporate power. Every major event
in history is a result of at least one conspiracy if not many! People
are always working in cahoots to get more money and power. Power
equals people working in cahoots, and getting people to believe
them. This is a fact no matter how much people want to lie to
themselves. The founding fathers creating America against the
wishes of England = conspiracy. Lenin and Trotsky over throwing
the Russian Crown = conspiracy. War of the Roses = an orgy of
conspiracy. Jesus being railed roaded by his fellow Jews and killed
by the Roman state = biggest conspiracy story in history.

To think we don't have powerful people conspiring today
equates to a denial of history, reality, and nonworking brain. All of
human history is a story of a small amount of people figuring out a
way to fuck over everyone else. Conspiracies are a fact of life, the
only way to kill conspiracy is demanding transparency.
Transparency acts as a disinfectant. That is why Wikileaks and
Edward Snowden are viewed as such a threat to the establishment. It
erodes the power of secrecy by forcing transparency. Our current
status is polar opposite of what it should be, an open government and
private citizens. Instead, we have a secretive government and spied
on citizens. Roll the rampant PC movement into the mix, and that's
the formula for oppression.

If you're interested in unfounded conspiracies that involve
Illuminati human sacrifices, reptilian shape shifting royalty, and
polaroid's of George Bush and John Kerry butt-fucking each other at

a Skull and Bones ceremony at Yale University you're going to be disappointed. Bush or Kerry? Who's the bottom? Answer: Probably Kerry, he lost the election in 2004.

How we've been getting played...

The notion of powerful people using less powerful people to extend their wealth and power has been around for thousands of years. Being a noble warrior was therefore promoted by the ruling class in society. Why? 1) An ass kicking warrior pledged to do your bidding was an extension of your own power. 2) His ass kicking is going to result in the accumulation of more wealth and power. Normally, the common people do not want to fight unless it's viewed as a defensive measure. Of course historically there are exceptions like the Vikings. At least their looting was honest in intent and they shared in the spoils. The message to Viking society was fairly clear, fuck those other guys. Let's take their shit and make slaves out of the ones we didn't kill. This is the plan: we're getting on this boat, sailing to England, rape, kill, pillage, and sail back home where we will be treated like heroes.

In modern history the intent has been camouflaged under a layer of disinformation and pushing pseudo-patriotism. Most people want to be left alone. Think about it, what interaction have you had with the government that is pleasant? For most people that would be a fat goose egg. That is definitely the mindset shared my most Americans and people across the world. However, these entities keep growing larger and larger, directing more and more aspects of life. How does that make any fucking sense? I've been across this country and all over the world. We all view killing as wrong, and do not want our young being killed or injured in rich men's wars. We all want to be free. We would like to see our tax money going to more useful endeavors than killing people. As a country we need to ask ourselves what the hell is going on? Why are we provided with such little information which is always incomplete or spun. Think about the recent events in Benghazi, and the misinformation. Or the reasoning to invade Iraq? Our history is plagued by this horrible pattern which must stop if we want to leave this world a better place for our children. The best way to perceive the present is understanding the past. We need to understand history which goes beyond the reductionist storyline we are spoon fed in school. We need to understand stand current events beyond the mainstream narrative which for some strange reason always leaves out who's making all the damn money. Thinking harder never heart anyone except for those who are in the wrong.

Spanish American War

In 1896 corporations directly purchased their first presidential election. The race was between Republican William McKinley and Populist back Democrat William Jennings Bryan. The Populist Party emerged because people were critical of the power and influence the robber barons had within the economic and political spheres. They were seeing more and more influence being shifted to the desires of the elite away from the common man. Populist Democrat Bryan had a budget of $600,000 to spend on the campaign. While McKinley's campaign had corporate donations reached $3.5 million. With those millions of dollars his campaign was able to hire hundreds of trained speakers, millions of posters, billboards, and 300,000,000 flyers in nine languages.

At the turn of the 20th century Spain ruled Cuba which by the 19th century became the richest colony because of its sugar production. Rockefeller's National City Bank wanted Cuba's sugar production as an addition to its holdings of Standard Oil. *The New York Journal* owned by William Hurst began bombarding Americans with horrible stories of Spanish oppression. The stories included Spaniards feeding people to sharks, roasting priests, and killing hospital patients where there weren't any hospitals. During this period of time there was a battle of newspapers also happening between Hurst and Joseph Pulitzer. As a result they sensationalized journalism to the point it lost touch with reality just to sell papers and carry favor with people who wanted to influence public opinion. The term "yellow press" was coined. Ironic, how Pulitzer is associated to excellence in journalism when he printed a lot of crap. McKinley's White House decided to get involved. During a secret White House meeting, it was decided to send a ship called the Maine to Cuba. The Spanish government wasn't expecting any visitors when it showed up in Havana Harbor. Captain Charles Sigsbee of the Maine noted, "It became known to me after word that Maine had not been expect even by the United State Council General." Even though it showed up without warning Spain permitted the main to dock for three weeks.

In the meantime, the "yellow press" kept pumping out false stories to drive public outrage to war. Hurst paid bribes to have the Spanish Ambassador's correspondence spied upon. One of the letters of the Spanish Ambassador was critical of McKinley. Reasonable, they did just parked a warship in your harbor and are making threatening gestures. However, Hurst framed it as the worst insult to America in its history. Two days later the Maine exploded in Havana Harbor.

On board the destroyed ship 266 men were killed. A US Navy Court of Inquiry attributed the explosion to an external device such as a torpedo or a bomb, but was unable to assign blame. As you can guess, the "yellow press" blamed the Spanish Government. With sensationalized stories and provoking illustrations the American public was driven into war with the battle cry of "Remember the Maine". Now we can be the saviors of the oppressed colonies of Spain and pay them back for sinking our ship. It's important to remember the last thing Spain would want is a war with the US. It would make as much sense for Spain to attack us now as it did then. There was no question in their mind they would get their asses handed to them, they were still using wood ships. In fact, all Spanish documents show Spain wanted to avoid war with America at all costs. Out gunned with inferior technology it was a one side battle of US dominance. One Naval victory after the next. US victories and stories about Teddy Roosevelt and his rough riders charging up San Juan Hill resonated in the public's mind as they read their newspapers which lead to his popularity and eventual rise to president.

However, the question still remains how did the Maine really blow up? The three likely culprits are:

1. Contrary to all evidence and logic Spain did it.

2. Mechanical failure, such as a boiler blowing up. There have been four major inquires to the explosion. The first three from the military, and the last in by the National Geographic Society. The first investigation by the US Navy Court of Inquiry attributed it to a mine situated under the bottom of the ship. The second investigation in 1911 by the Army Corps of Engineer built a cofferdam around the wreckage and pumped it out. They concluded the sinking was due to a mine. The third inquiry in 1974 the Navy reinvestigated, but this time came to the conclusion that the cause of sinking

was internal. The fourth investigation came in 1999 and was conducted by the National Geographic Society. NGS commissioned a study by Advanced Marine Enterprises, which conducted the first detailed computer modeling of the disaster. AME stated that a coal fire within a bunker could have raised the temperature within one of the Maine's magazines to hazardous levels within a few hours. As to a mine strike, AME found that even a simple mine consisting of 100 pounds of black powder and a contact fuse could have sunk the ship. "If so, the mine must have been perfectly placed, which under the circumstances would have been as much a matter of luck as skill." While it did not discount either option for the Maine's destruction, AME ultimately concluded (based on the 1911 photographs) that there was more evidence in favor of the Maine's destruction by a mine.

3. With most of the evidence leading away from Spain and mechanical failure. Who would benefit? Any detective knows you follow the money. To help finance the war the Rockefeller's National City Bank loaned the US government $250 million dollars. Today that would be over $6.5 billion. Income tax in those days did not exist. In order to repay the loan the telephone use tax was levied on the American people. This tax reminded in effect for over a century. The loan was negotiated by Assistant Treasurer Secretary Frank Vanderlab, after the war National City Bank made Vanderlab its president. The cronyism has been going on a long time folks. As the National City Bank president he later took part in creating the Federal Reserve when he and other banking heads secretly met at Jekyle Island off the coast of Georgia. Mark Twain believed the reason for the war was

money interests that wanted to obtain the sugar production when he stated:

"How our hearts burned with indignation against the atrocious Spaniards... But when the smoke was over, the dead buried and the cost of the war came back to the people in an increase in the price of commodities and rent - that is, when we sobered up from our patriotic spree - it suddenly dawned on us that the cause of the Spanish-American War was the price of sugar." -Mark Twain

The Rockefeller National City Bank directly benefited greatly from the war. Soon after the War, Cuba became dotted with National City Bank branches while it was taking over the Cuban sugar industry. Major General Smedley Butler was, at the time of his death (1940), the most decorated Marine in American history. In his book *War is a Racket* stated bluntly:

"I have spent 34 years in active service as a member of the Marine Corps. And during that period I spent most of my time being a high-class muscle man for big business, for Wall Street and for the bankers. In short, I was a racketeer for capitalism. I helped make Mexico safe for American oil interests in 1914. I helped make Haiti and Cuba a decent place for the National City Bank to collect revenues." -Major General Smedley Butler

This was the first war we fought which introduced the idea that we should go fight on other peoples' behalf rather than just national defense. This feeling of moral obligation was manipulated by lies printed by Hurst and Pulitzer. The good hearted American people honestly believed the fabricated stories they were reading, and wanted to help the downtrodden Cubans. By pulling the on the heart strings of the American people big business and banking profited off financing the war, and reaping it's spoils. No matter the direction of approach to the totality of events leading up to war, this by definition is a false flag. False Flag is defined covert operations that are designed to deceive in such a way that the operations appear as though they are being carried out by entities, groups, or nations other than those who actually planned and executed them. The only way one could argue this wasn't a fucked up false flag is denying the existence of factional historical elements, and/or the actual meaning of words. This is a psychological condition of denialism, a person's choice to deny reality as a way to avoid psychologically uncomfortable truths.

Granted, false flag is a difficult term because it's a loaded term. People have been conditioned to believe that those two words together, "false" and "flag" are woo-woo and ridiculed. Do you trust the government? Would government lie, when people in government are proven to be pathological liars? Nothing to see here move along, let's classify the records. Its historical fact, America has used false flags to influence the masses like a bunch of stupid sheep. Even after all this, the people of Cuba were still treated as surfs on their own island.

To recap this exchange between We the People vs. Establishment effects of this war.

We the People:
Lied to.
A new telephone tax to pay for the war that went on for 100 years.
American deaths :3289 battle and disease related.
Spanish Deaths: approx 55000-60000 battle and disease related.
More National Debt

*In real terms this is an all-around loss for everyday Americans.

Establishment:
Collected money as return on investment from financing the war.
Acquired an already operational extremely lucrative sugar industry.
Sold more papers by printing lies.
Elite Deaths: 0
*This is what we like to call a "win-win."

Through this paradigm, if we look at the exchange of every war through history this same pattern emerges. Regardless of side there are no real winners in war except the elite who control military industrial war complex and finance. Who died, indebted, and suffered vs who profited is the real score card in War. This understating transcends "we beat the Spanish", and more accurately describes true score card.

Hegelian Dialectic

This formula for people in power to stay in power and get more has been around of a long long long time. Create a problem or use an existing problem. Invoke fear. Offer solution that benefits you which costs the masses their independence and prosperity. Result amplifies your power. When people are in fear, there is a psychological response of a cry for protection. HELP ME! "Dependency head fuck" should be the proper terminology for this modus operandi; however, it's called the Hegelian Dialectic after the German philosopher Georg Wilhelm Friedrich Hegel. Is made up of three parts.

1) Thesis - Problem.
2) Antithesis - Reaction
3) Synthesis - Solution.

Creating the idea of enemy or fear in the minds of people allows the people in power to amplify their power over their minions. It has been this way since the beginning of recorded history. The underlying reason: knowledge is power. When you create the rules of the game, you are not bound by the psychological effects of the game play and the production of fear. This is why crazy cult leaders and the ruling class have a separate set of rules for their followers, do as I say not as I do. In *The Wealth of Nations*, Adam Smith remarked:

"Fear is in almost all cases a wretched instrument of government, and ought in particular never to be employed against any order of men who have the smallest pretensions to independency." –Adam Smith

Let's look a couple of examples of the Hegelian Dialectic philosophy. This political philosophical paradox in a lot of ways is analogous with Chinese finger traps. The initial reaction of the people is fear which forces a reaction to pull outward which only tightens the trap. Fear is a mind killer. If we can relax, be mindful, and demand pertinent information we can accept the reality of situation, and figure out how to get out of the trap.

CHURCH

We see it displayed in various religious organizations for centuries.

PROBLEM: Everyone is scared of dying, and the sadness of missing loved ones who've passed. Play on the fear of dying and going to hell.

REACTION: The church gives people a formula to follow which they are told insures salvation and makes the people feel secure. You go to hell if you don't follow the formula. To be fair to churches, they do offer some good values and community which is an important element in civic virtue (social fabric, shared ideals), but there are some strings attached. Group think/Social Proof also is at play.

SOLUTION: Now you have a group of people convinced of a formula which gives power to a priest class, or whoever is in charge. The people are convinced of the formula, any logical issues with the formula are met with cognitive dissonance because it erodes the false sense of security. This is why churches have so much money, the formula always includes giving them your money. Honestly people, if there is an intelligent God of creation which created everything in universe do you really think he gave power to charlatans to do your thinking for you? I've always wondered if the underlying purpose for sacrifice in ancient times was to give the priests good meat for their sacrificial BBQs. It's a great ratchet if that was really the case.

GOVERNMENT

There are a lot of examples, here is a recent example.

PROBLEM: Play on the fear of the 9-11 attacks. Regardless of the cause, inside job or not, fear was amplified among the masses who no longer felt secure.

REACTION: Under the guise of making us feel more secure. The federal government responded in multiple ways expanding its power and influence in the name of terrorism.

SOLUTION: One of many solutions which the government usurped more control was the NSA's wiring tapping and the bullshit TSA at the airports. Now the government has the ability to track and monitor its own citizens contrary to the Bill of Rights - the right to privacy. They also have the ability to control citizen's movements through the TSA. More framework of control is set in place to control the domestic enemy. This is some real Orwellian shit. Mass surveillance and "papers please" is a hallmark of tyranny. This is something which has been in the works for a while, and a goal of those in control. Zbigniew Brzezinski: National Security Advisor under the Carter Administration, CFR member, Bilderburg attendee, co-founder with David Rockefeller of the Trilateral Commission, and advisor to President Obama illustrated the coming world of surveillance in American Society in his 1970 book *Between Two Ages: America's Role in the Technetronic Era* he wrote:

"The technotronic era involves the gradual appearance of a more controlled society. Such a society would be dominated by an elite, unrestrained by traditional values. Soon it will be possible to assert almost continuous surveillance over every citizen and maintain up-to-date complete files containing even the most personal information about the citizen. These files will be subject to instantaneous retrieval by the authorities."

Either Zbigniew Brzezinski is a seer, or this been in the works for a while... Traditional values is a very important topic to

179

consider. It is moral codes and beliefs passed down from one generation to the next. Traditional values of family, liberty for all, honesty, and free speech are all being jeopardized by this ever growing powerful elite as Brzezinski commented. We see the societal ramifications of this influence taking place today. The PC censorship movement is a product of this social engineering. He should know, he is one of the unelected elite who has been determining US policy for decades.

World War I

Norman Dodd, former director of the Committee to Investigate Tax Exempt Foundations of the U.S. House of Representatives, testified that the Committee was invited to study the minutes of the Carnegie Endowment for International Peace as part of the Committee's investigation. The Committee stated:

"The trustees of the Foundation brought up a single question. If it is desirable to alter the life of an entire people, is there any means more efficient than war.... They discussed this question... for a year and came up with an answer: There are no known means more efficient than war, assuming the objective is altering the life of an entire people. That leads them to a question: How do we involve the United States in a war. This is in 1909." -Normon Dodd ,US House of Representatives

The consensus among the elites was that the US should enter a war around the around the time of WWI. In 1915 World War I was underway. Britain was at war with Germany, and the US still had not gotten involved. At the time the public, statesmen, and senators didn't want to get involved in a costly war that would demand lives.

Even though Wilson proclaimed America's neutrality in the European War, his government was secretly plotting to involve the American people by having the Lusitania sunk. This was made public in the book *The Intimate Papers of Colonel House*, written by a supporter of the Colonel, who recorded a conversation between Colonel House and Sir Edward Grey of England, the Foreign Secretary of England. Grey asks, "What will America do if the Germans sink an ocean liner with American passengers on board?" to which House responds, "I believe that a flame of indignation would sweep the United States and that by itself would be sufficient to carry us into the war." This is the same Edward M. House (CFR) which was the banking elite's puppet master of Woodrow Wilson for two terms, was one of a handful of powerful men who met secretly to create the Federal Reserve, and was instrumental in the creation of the Council on Foreign Relations.

England broke the German communications war code on December 14, 1914, so the English a fairly good idea where the U-boats were located. This meant that the First Lord of the Admiralty, Winston Churchill, knew where every U-boat was in the vicinity of the English Channel that separated England and France. The ocean liner Lusitania was set to sail from the US to England. Prior to its departure, the German government had placed advertisements in the New York newspapers warning the American people considering travel. The basic message was ships heading to England were sailing into a war zone, and could be sunk. The main reason for this was because munitions were being sent via ocean liners to support Britain in the War. Bad time to take a cruise, the public was unaware of the onboard munitions. Plus in people's minds sinking such an impressive ship seemed impossible. Secretary of State William Jennings Bryan promised that he would endeavor to persuade the President publicly to warn the Americans not to travel. No such warning was issued by the President, but there can be no doubt that President Wilson was told of cargo destined for the Lusitania. He did nothing... In fact, after the sinking the ship's manifest was hidden away in the archives of the US Treasury. Secretary Bryan resigned from his post as a result of how President Wilson handled the Lusitania affair.

On May 7, 1915, the Lusitania was sunk off the coast of County Cork, Ireland by a U-boat after it had slowed to await the arrival of the English escort vessel, the Juno. The Juno never arrived, and the Lusitania sat alone in the channel. 1201 people lost their lives in the sinking, over 120 of them American. Colin Simpson, the author of a book *The Lusitania*, described it as "the foulest act of willful murder ever committed on the seas." The Los Angeles Times reviewed Simpson's book and concluded: "*The Lusitania* proves beyond a reasonable doubt that the British government connived at the sinking of the passenger ship in order to lure America into World War I. The Germans, whose torpedo struck the liner, were the unwitting accomplices or victims of a plot probably concocted by Winston Churchill."

When President Wilson was seeking re-election in 1916. He campaigned on his record of "keeping us out of the War" during his first term of office from 1912 to 1916 while doing just the opposite behind closed doors. This act of foul play against the American public set the backdrop for entering WWI. It was a premise built by lies. By manipulating and pulling the strings behind the scenes, big business and banking interests were ready to make a windfall at the expense of the common tax payer. This same cycle of evil exploitation has been happening for over 100 years. This side of history is not taught in school, for one reason. History is written by the winners, and in this case it's the elite. Notice how the financial part of war is never spoken about.

Arguably one of the best 20th century financial journalist who studied the history of America's wealth and power was Ferdinand Lundberg (1902-1995). He was a highly esteemed specialist in financial reporting, was an adjunct professor of social philosophy at New York University. In his book *America's Sixty Families (1937)*, he clearly illustrates who made the money and how in World War I. Since the Lundberg tells the story so well and to the point, his book will be heavily quoted.

"As revealed in 1936 by the Nye Senate Committee, Secretary of State William Jennings Bryan on August 10, 1914, less than two weeks after war began, informed President Wilson that J. P. Morgan and Company had inquired whether there would be any official objection to making a loan to the French government through the Rothschilds. Bryan warned the President that "money is the worst of all contrabands," and that if the loan were permitted, the interests of the powerful persons making it would be enlisted on the side of the borrower, making neutrality difficult, if not impossible." It's important to note that upon the death of J.P. Morgan, a rich man, but his personal was worth a great deal less than perceived. The vast major of the money he was using belonged to the Rothschild's banking family. *"On August 15 Bryan wrote to J. P. Morgan and Company, "Loans made by American bankers to any foreign nation which is at war are inconsistent with the true spirit of neutrality." This statement formally committed the United States against loans to warring Europe. Soon afterward Bryan was constrained to reverse himself, which he did privately."* The flood gates of financing were officially open for Bankers Trust Company (J.P Morgan) and National City Bank (Rockefeller) to make a killing.

"Early in 1917 the Allied governments, which now owed the American bankers and their clients nearly $1,500,000,000, had been

brought virtually to their knees by the German armies, and it was
believed that the limit of Allied credit had been reached. In March,
1917, the Czar's government, which had also been fighting to make
the world safe for democracy, collapsed, threatening to release the
German army of the East for duty in France." The bankers were
afraid that Germany was actually going to win. If that happened
money would be lost, and not made. They wouldn't be able to collect
interest from a government that no longer exists. No France = No
Money. The secret to winning a war if you are a bank is to have no
real winners. Lend both sides money, they fight it out for a while,
and then profit off the blood money. When the populations are done
fighting they are more indebted and you get to collect more money
from the tax payer. In addition to the money made from lending to
governments at war, profits were had from the real goods supplied
by the companies owned by these banking interests. A detailed
financial inspection of war shows its nothing more than a massive
murderous profiting making endeavor for a few.

    "On March 5, 1917, Walter Hines Page, American
Ambassador to England, sent to President Wilson a long dispatch
which Page summarized as follows: "I think that the pressure of this
approaching crisis has gone beyond the ability of the Morgan
Financial Agency for the British and French Governments. The need
is becoming too great and urgent for any private agency to meet, for
every such agency has to encounter jealousies of rivals and of
sections." Page said that the outlook was "alarming" to America's
industrial and financial prospects, but pointed out frankly, "If we
should go to war with Germany, the greatest help we could give the
Allies would be such a credit. In that case our Government could, if
it would, make a large investment in a Franco-British loan or might
guarantee such a loan.... Unless we go to war with Germany our
Government, of course, cannot make such a direct grant of credit

......" The alternative to war, Page warned, was domestic collapse. Within four weeks President Wilson asked Congress for a declaration of war, and promptly acceded."

"Out of the proceeds of the very first Liberty Loan more than $400,000,000 was paid to J. P. Morgan and Company in satisfaction of debts owed it by the British government! During its participation in the war the United States lent to Europe $9,386,311,178, of which Great Britain got $4,136,000,000 and France $2,293,000,000. American participation in the war made it possible for the government to place the credit of the whole American people behind the Allies, whose fortunes were, early in 1917, at such a low ebb that the American holders of nearly $1,500,000,000 of English and French paper stood to suffer a disastrous loss. The declaration of war by the United States, in addition to extricating the wealthiest American families from a dangerous situation, also opened new vistas of profits." By the end of the Wilson Administration national debt increased by 800% all payable to the banks who got the US into the war in the first place. Here is an example of the banks speculating to make themselves more rich and powerful, us paying for their mistakes, and them laughing all the way to the bank. Our grandparents or great-grandparents bailed them out by assuming their debt. The same thing happened in 2008 bail-out when we assumed their debt in the housing crisis.

"Europe got none of the money lent by the Treasury; it received only materials of war. The owners of American industries got the money. They employed most of it to expand the industrial equipment of the nation and to increase the size of their fortunes and the extent of their power. In short, the war debt created by the American government amounted simply to money transferred from the people of the country to the richest families, who owned the banks and industries." Today the money still is channeled in the

same directions although the root the money travels is move convoluted it's still getting to the same places. Away from the people and to the elite. We need to ask ourselves upon what factual information are people convinced the war is good for the economy? That is some serious brainwashing propaganda. We can spend massive amounts on other things that don't kill people and make the elite wealthier. This delusion needs to end before more people needlessly die at the hands of these psycho-paths.

This brings us to the point of the creation of the Council on Foreign Relations. The financial elites from America and Europe, the same folks responsible for the Spanish War and exploiting the American public in World War I came together formally to create a "think tank". This entity, and later in concert with the Trilateral Commission has driven every major US policy since the First World War. There policy making, war mongering, and profiteering is alive and well today. In fact, they probably are at the pinnacle of their power. The only thing in their way is us, the unwashed masses, who need to get informed.

History of the CFR

Arguably one of the best historians in the last century was a man by the name of Carroll Quigley. He was a professor of history and theorist of the evolution of civilization. He received his B.A., M.A., and Ph.D. degree from Harvard University. He taught at various Ivy League schools; Princeton University, Harvard, and at the School of Foreign Service at Georgetown University. In addition to his academic work he consulted for various government entities: US Department of Defense, US Navy, Smithsonian Institution, and the House Select Committee on Astronautics and Space Exploration. In the 1960's Quigley was given permission to examine the papers and records of the Council on Foreign Relations for the purpose of writing their own internal history. He later came out with the book *Tragedy & Hope*, where he shows that:

"The powers of financial capitalism has another far reaching aim nothing less than to create a world system of financial control in the private hands able to dominate the political system of each country and the economy of the world as a whole." Carroll Quigley PhD

Now this is not a book about conspiracy, it's a book about reality. Bill Clinton regarded him as one of his biggest influences. If we can agree the powers of financial capitalism controls government, we agree - it looks like a duck. If the people who are part of this oligarchy are members of the same club, and are talking with each other in closed meetings and always lying to the public - it talks like a duck. If they are benefiting from controlled moves in business, military, and government - it walks like a duck. Can we agree if it looks like a duck, talks like duck, and walks like a duck, it's a fucking duck? If politicians are puppets of the financial elite, we should find out whose hands are up their asses.

"Forget the politicians. The politicians are put there to give you the idea that you have freedom of choice. You don't. You have no choice. You have owners. They own you. They own everything. They own all the important land. They own and control the corporations. They've long since bought and paid for the Senate, the Congress, the state houses, the city halls. They got the judges in their back pockets and they own all the big media companies, so they control just about all of the news and information you get to hear. They got you by the balls. They spend billions of dollars every year lobbying. Lobbying to get what they want." -George Carlin

Many regard Quigley's history as a conspiratorial view of history as explained by the conspirators themselves. Quigley was very close to the CRF and the Roundtable Group, in fact he said he was invited into its inner circle and was given the opportunity of examining its records. He was considered to be the official historian of this group. He admired it, thought it was wonderful, and agreed with their aims. The main disagreement he had with the group was the secrecy in which it operated. He did not agree that its ambitions should be hidden from view. He wrote a couple of books about this group, *Tragedy and Hope* and the *Anglo-American Establishment.* He felt that with all these years of success in their ambitious movement it was time to come forward, show what it had accomplished, and openly proclaim its goals.

Tragedy and Hope, and the *Anglo American Establishment* are like most history books, very dry. However, they are extremely well thought out and rich with detailed information. Quigley did an excellent job of combining the elements of society which drives it through time. He takes into consideration economics, religion, ruling structures, education, and etc. when explaining history. These books were not written for mass consumption, they were written for academia and for people who are part of groups such as the CFR. Even though it was a dry history book, people started to read it because information within its pages alarmed people.

Why did it alarm people? Because the history of the power establishment was so well documented. The book *Tragedy and Hope* caused a stir and the book publisher McMillan & Company stopped publishing claiming there wasn't a market for it. In fact there was a large market for this book, pirated copies of it emerged, and 1000's of pirated copies were sold. Luckily for us, it has been back in print for years because of demand and we can buy a copy.

After a thoughtful person reads *Tragedy and Hope* or *Anglo-American Establishment,* three things will likely happen:

1. The world will make a lot more sense.
2. You are going to want to stop the direction we are heading.
3. If you are a moral person with a backbone, you'll probably be pissed.

According to Quigley, at the end of the 19th century a secret society was created in England by Cecil Rhodes. Cecil Rhodes was one of the wealthiest men in the world. He was the chancellor of South Africa, and owned almost all of the gold and diamond minds of South Africa.

Cecil Rhode created five wills and very specifically instructed how to spend his wealth. In short, he said that it should be used for the purpose of creating a secret society. One of the wills created the Rhodes Scholarship. He set aside this money for the education of young people. However, its main goal was the farm team from which to recruit people into this global governance movement. The other wills are not very well known. This movement Rhodes created, which includes the CRF, has been a major historical force since World War I. According to Quigley, every major event since World War I has been dominated and directed by a large extent by this underlying force. The original design of this group was to expand the British Empire's culture and political system and control the entire world.

Not too surprising, if you consider that's what they had been doing openly for centuries. Like a vindictive Ex, they wanted to fuck with their newly freed boyfriend or girlfriend. Many elites at that time thought it was a shame the US left England. Rhodes felt the English represented the best culture, most evolved race, and the very best in the world. They had an obligation to rule the world whether or not people liked it, accept this way of life by hook or by crook.

This is the same kind of superiority thinking that has been used when forcing most ideologies: Christianity, Islam, Capitalism, and Communism. Either you're getting forced or tricked into something which results in someone having power over you. This idea evolved very quickly after Cecil Rhodes death because the world was continuing to change. Instead of the British Empire's supremacy at the center of power within movement a world government or system of control would be created.

They understood in order to control the masses they had to control the organizations to which they belonged. The power centers of society. One thing that is clear is that we have herd instincts. Human kind has tribal instincts ingrained into its DNA. Organizations play to our tribal instincts which yearns for community. They understand the human condition of group think. If you want to have control of the masses you capture control of the leadership of various groups. Political parties, education, labor, media, and corporations can be control by a fairly small amount of people via financial means. This model was established, and it is the model that governs the world today and is the reason why we have an oligarchy.

According to Quigley, the structure that Cecil Rhodes developed was modeled after the Jesuit Order. He established an organizational structure of rings within rings within rings. What that means is at the center there is a small number of people, around them larger organizational rings are formed which takes direction from the smaller ring. By this method information can be compartmentalized which leverages informational control. Somebody on an outer ring may not be onboard with the ideas being pushed if they understood the totality of what was going on in reality. For example, CFR members Katie Kureg or Angela Jolie would not be privy to the same level of information as Zbigniew Brezezinski (CFR) or Henry

Kissinger (CFR) when hatching policy decisions with whoever is the active Secretary of State or CIA director who's also just so happens to be a CFR member. Also, having some of this publicly liked people as window dressing on the outer ring gives the group a less threatening appearance.

The other inherent benefit to the rings within rings structure is plausible deniability if shit goes sideways when doing something underhanded. If the group gets accused of something which members are responsible for they can roll out people who are just there as decoration to talk. This serves as protection to the overall group because public sentiment would be split and nothing will get done. In fact, the first time the term "plausible deniability" was used in public was by Allen Dulles (CFR) head of the CIA and director of the Council on Foreign Relations. This methodology is actively used in government intelligence and military around the world. The society Rhodes originally named was called the Society of the Elect. Ironic, because they run the world unelected, but self-elected.

They established Round Table Groups which still exist to this day. Associated to the Round Table Groups were established the Royal Institute of International Affair (UK), and in the US it is called the Council on Foreign Relations. He recruited a small number of highly place influential people from British banking and politics to get this movement started.

As time went on the center of power within this movement shifted geographically from London to New York. The League of Nations which morphed into United Nations was conceived by this group. The main idea was to control the levers of government from behind the scenes, and not the politicians. Funny how comedian George Carlin and respected historian Carol Quigley are saying the same damn thing, they are our owners. They were the ones that would select and fund the political figures. After almost 100 years of existence they are close to controlling the whole world, A New World Order. CFR member, Former Secretary of State Henry Kissinger, and one of the principle architects of US forging policy for decades had this to say:

"Today, America would be outraged if U.N. troops entered Los Angeles to restore order. Tomorrow they will be grateful! This is especially true if they were told that there were an outside threat from beyond, whether real or promulgated, that threatened our very existence. It is then that all peoples of the world will plead to deliver them from this evil. The one thing every man fears is the unknown. When presented with this scenario, individual rights will be willingly relinquished for the guarantee of their well-being granted to them by the World Government." –Dr. Henry Kissinger, Evians France 1991

Notice the use of the Hegelian Dialectic in that quote. He's spelling out the modus operandi they've been using for decades. Wake up, they are one trick ponies that leverage fear to accomplish their goals which cost you your freedom and wealth. The United States has been bankrolling and enforcing this movement via our military. Quigley wrote in "Tragedy and Hope":

"The chief problem of American political life ...has been how to make the two Congressional parties more national and international. The argument that the two parties should represent opposed ideals and policies, one, perhaps, of the Right and the other of the Left, is a foolish idea acceptable only to doctrinaire and academic thinkers. Instead, the two parties should be almost identical, so that the American people can 'throw the rascals out' at any election without leading to any profound or extensive shifts in policy." - Carol Quigley

Republican or Democrat doesn't matter. Coke or Pepsi, either way you're drinking brown corn syrup water. Quigley not knowing

192

what to call the entity at large referred to it as the network because there was no name. If you want to keep a large movement secret you don't fucking name it. I know what some maybe saying bullshit, or WTF? Cognitive dissonance making your head ring that something like this exists? Remember embrace it, keep learning, don't shut down. At least at the end of your research, you'll have learned something, and come to a semblance of truth of the crazy world we live in. You'll understand **why** and **how** things got fucked up, and **why** they are not getting better. Newspaper columnist and granddaughter of US President Theodore Roosevelt had the following to report on the subject in *Indianapolis News* in 1961.

"The word 'Establishment' is a general term for the power elite in international finance, business, the professions and government, largely from the northeast, who wield most of the power regardless of who is in the White House. Most people are unaware of the existence of this 'legitimate Mafia.' Yet the power of the Establishment makes itself felt from the professor who seeks a foundation grant, to the candidate for a cabinet post or State Department job. It affects the nation's policies in almost every area... What is the Establishment's view-point? Through the Roosevelt, Truman, Eisenhower and Kennedy administrations its ideology is constant: That the best way to fight Communism is by a One World Socialist state governed by 'experts' like themselves. The result has been policies which favor the growth of the super state, gradual surrender of United States sovereignty to the United Nations and a steady retreat in the face of Communist aggression." -Edith Kermit Roosevelt

Financing the Bolsheviks - Russia

What needs to be understood is that it's never been about ideology for the elite. There is no such thing as ideology, it's in your head. It's about power, and the elites understand this perfectly. Power over people is without ideology, might equals right. On a philosophical level manipulating ideological thinkers on a personal level or on a massive level is easy, their pressure points are obvious and weaknesses are obvious. It's analogous with a multidiscipline MMA fighter getting into the ring with someone who only knows how to throw punches. The puncher's ignorance is going to be used against him by the opponent who isn't bond by training that consists of only boxing. Ideologies of Fascism, Communism, and our current form of Neoliberal Capitalism culminates into the same beast – tyranny by a few over the many.

Being born in the late 1970's, I was a child of the 1980's. We always heard about the horrible Commies and how much they hated us because we were free. In school we learn about how the popular uprising of the Bolsheviks overthrowing the ruling class of the Tsars. NEVER, do you hear about who paid for the revolution. I studied Russian, took Russian history classes in university, and they never broached the topic of financing. Normally, regime changes or revolutions don't come cheap. They cost a lot of money. Propaganda, bribes, and weapons are not free. Hint. Hint. This is the reason there is a 2nd Amendment, right to bear arms, and the talk about armed state militias. A counter balance to tyranny which is self-contained among the population that doesn't rely on outside financing...

As we shall see the planning, the leadership, and especially the financing came entirely from outside Russia. Mostly from financiers in Germany, Britain and the United States. This story

194

begins with the war between Russia and Japan in 1904. Jacob Schiff (CFR), who was head of the New York investment firm Kuhn, Loeb and Company, had raised the capital for large war loans to Japan. He was one of the principal backers of the Bolshevik revolution. In 1905 the Mikado awarded Jacob Schiff a medal, the Second Order of the Treasure of Japan, in recognition of his important role in that campaign. Even 100 years ago banking interests and the CRF have been after the control of Russia. The foothold was backing communism to gain control over industry and commerce. Russia has been difficult for them to control. When Stalin took over, and as time progressed, he told them to go pound sand and the cold war materialized in an east vs west power struggle.

During the years of WWI, thousands of Russian soldiers were taken as prisoners. Sources outside of Russia, which were hostile to the Tsarist regime, paid for the printing of Marxist propaganda and had it delivered to the prison camps. Russian-speaking revolutionaries were trained in New York and sent to distribute the pamphlets among the prisoners and to indoctrinate the soldiers into rebellion against their own government. When the war was ended, these officers and enlisted men returned home to become virtual seeds of treason against the Tsar. They were to play a major role a few years later in creating mutiny among the military during the Communist takeover of Russia. This revolution was anything but organic as portrayed in history classes. It was orchestrated from on high.

One of the best known Russian revolutionaries at that time was Leon Trotsky. He and Lenin were the two figure heads of the revolution both linked to elite banking in Europe and America. In January of 1916 Trotsky was expelled from France and came to the United States. It has been claimed that his expenses were paid by Jacob Schiff (CFR). There is no documentation to substantiate that claim, but the circumstantial evidence does point to a wealthy donor in New York. According to Trotsky, on many occasions a chauffeured limousine was placed at his service by a wealthy friend, identified as Dr. M. Dr. M., could have been a man by the name of Max May who was a JP Morgan (CFR) New York banker who would later go on to be the director of the first Soviet formed bank in Moscow, Ruskombank.

On March 23, 1917 a mass meeting was held at Carnegie Hall to celebrate the abdication of Nicolas II, which meant the overthrow of Tsarist rule in Russia. Thousands of socialists, Marxists, nihilists and anarchists attended to cheer the event. The following day there was published on page two of the New York Times a telegram from Jacob Schiff, which had been read to this audience. He expressed regrets, that he could not attend and then described the successful Russian revolution as "...what we had hoped and striven for these long years". (Mayor Calls Pacifists Traitors, The New York Times, March 24, 1917, p. 2)

In the February 3, 1949 issue of the *New York Journal American* Schiff's grandson, John, was quoted by columnist Cholly Knickerbocker as saying that his grandfather had given about $20 million for the triumph of Communism in Russia. You need to ask yourself why is the world are these "capitalist" supporting communists? Hint, there is no such binding ideology for the elite. Think in terms of power and influence only, there is no such thing as binding ideology. Only ends justifies means.

When Trotsky returned to Petrograd in May of 1917 to organize the Bolshevik phase of the Russian Revolution, he carried $10,000 for travel expenses. That would be close to $190,000 today. Trotsky was arrested by Canadian naval personnel when the ship stopped over at Halifax. The money in his possession is now a matter of official record. Trotsky was recognized as a threat to the best interest of pretty much any country he was in.

"I am going back to Russia to overthrow the provisional government and stop the war with Germany." (A full report on this meeting had been submitted to the U.S. Military Intelligence. See Senate Document No. 62, 66th Congress, Report and Hearings of the Subcommittee on the Judiciary, United States Senate, 1919, Vol. II, p. 2680.) –Leon Trotsky

With this in mind, we have to wonder who are the mysterious forces both in England and the United States which intervened on Trotsky's behalf in Canada? Immediately telegrams started to come in, from an obscure attorney in New York City, the Canadian Deputy Postmaster-General, and even from a high-ranking British military officer. All inquiring into Trotsky's situation and urging his immediate release. The head of the British Secret Service in America at the time was Sir William Wiseman. Who as fate would have it occupied the apartment directly above the apartment of Edward Mandell House (CFR) and who had become fast friends with him. House advised Wiseman, that President Wilson (CFR puppet) wished to have Trotsky released. Wiseman advised his government and the British Admiralty issued orders on April 21st, that Trotsky was to be sent on his way.

It would be a mistake to conclude, that Jacob Schiff (CFR) and Mandell House (CFR) only players in this debacle. Trotsky could not have gone even as far as Halifax without having been granted an American passport and this was accomplished by the personal intervention of President Wilson. Professor Antony Sutton says, "President Woodrow Wilson was the fairy godmother, who provided Trotsky with a passport to return to Russia to "carry forward" the revolution... At the same time careful State Department bureaucrats, concerned about such revolutionaries entering Russia, were unilaterally attempting to tighten up passport procedures."

In Russia prior to and during the revolution many observed, British and American agents were everywhere. They were actively particularly in Petrograd, providing money for insurrection. The subsequent publication of various memoirs and documents made it clear, that this funding was provided by Milner's Roundtable (connected to the CRF) and channeled through Sir George Buchanan, who was the British Ambassador to Russia at the time. Round Table members were working both sides of the conflict to weaken and topple the target government. Normally, you'd consider this treason because England was partnered with Russia fighting against Germany. However, the vision and scope of the war is much larger when you consider the people really calling the shots. Yet the British Ambassador himself represented the hidden group, which was financing the regime's downfall. This chess game has been going on for years, and people have been making plans which are multiple moves ahead of what the public and even those in government perceive.

Members of the CFR devised a plan considerably more ingenious, philanthropy to push the revolution. They came in disguised as Red Cross, officials on a humanitarian mission. The idea of philanthropy by the elites is nothing more than a way to move society in the direction they want. Wolves in sheep's clothing. The group consisted almost entirely of financiers, lawyers and accountants from New York banks and investment houses. The entire expense of the Red Cross Mission in Russia, including the purchase of uniforms, was paid for by the man, who was appointed by President Wilson to become its head, "Colonel" William Boyce

Thompson (CFR). According to Hermann Hagedorn, Thompson's biographer:

"He deliberately created the kind of setting, which would be expected of an American magnate: established himself in a suite in the Hotel de l'Europe, bought a French limousine, went dutifully to receptions and teas and evinced an interest in objects of art. Society and the diplomats, noting that here was a man of parts and power, began to flock about him. He was entertained at the embassies, at the houses of Kerensky's ministers. It was discovered, that he was a collector and those with antiques to sell fluttered around him offering him miniatures, Dresden china, tapestries, even a palace or two."

Thompson made it possible for the purchase on Wall Street of Russian bonds in the amount of ten million rubles. He gave two million rubles to socialist of the provisional government lead by Aleksandr Kerensky for propaganda purposes inside Russia. While J.P. Morgan (CFR) was giving money to the Bolsheviks. Bankers in cahoots, funding both sides again. It's hard to lose that way. Starting in 1918 and ending 1920, the US sent troops to Siberia to stave off any encroachment from Japan during the Russian Revolution. Japan saw Russia's revolution an opportunity to spread its influence further into Siberia. However, this was not what the elites wanted even though they originally financed Japan's war with Tsarist Russia. Now they wanted to protect their revolutionary investment. As a result, CFR's puppet President Woodrow Wilson sent 8000 US troops to the interior of Russia, 189 US soldiers died from all causes during this episode.

As illustrated in Professors Sutton books, western investment into Soviet Russia was massive. In fact, they could not have been the cold war enemy we were all raised to fear had this technology and money transfer never happened. Companies such as: Ford, AEG, GE, and Metropolitan-Vickers controlled by the elite and CFR members were major operators in the development of the Soviet industrial complex. The general design and supervision of construction, and much of the supply of equipment for the gigantic plants built between 1929 and 1933 was provided by Albert Kahn, Inc., of Detroit, the then most famous of U.S. industrial architectural firm. In fact, the first 5 year plan was written by Western Companies. Shocking I know. The paper trail goes back to US finance and industrialist. The promoted myth says it was Stalin's plan. No, it was a US corporate sponsored plan Stalin used. Russia, was so ass backwards there is no way they could have industrialized so fast without major help from the West. The biggest reason they were defunct after the Revolution is they killed most of the smart people if they weren't lucky enough to have escaped. This western evolvement played directly into the massive arms race which further empowered the elite at the expense of the common man and fighting around the globe.

As a result of the revolution (1917-1922) an estimated 9 million people died. Later, during Stalin's regime of terror 20 million perished. All this death and pain can be linked to people who were part of the various round-table groups including the CFR. The foothold banking and the elite wanted in Russia by backing communism to gain control over industry cost almost unfathomable suffering.

Russia Today

Now it appears with Putin in charge, the CFR and their minions are trying again to gain control of Russia. As we now see, tensions and propaganda are being ramped up in the media on both sides. Normally, this is the elite broadcasting what is to come, priming the population to be outraged to justify armed conflict. One thing the average American does not understand is that most Russian are aware of the Western elite's intrusion into their lives for the past 100 years. This is a bear we do not want to poke, there is no need to, and the outcome could be cataclysmic. The only reason to engage hostilely with them is to fulfil the wet dream of the elites who want control of its people and vast resources. The suffering that comes from conflict and war for most Americans is an abstract concept that has been glorified in movies. The loss, the fear, and suffering of losing between 7 to 20 million people in a war fought during their parent's or grandparent's generation on their soil is anything but abstract in the Russian psyche.

The escalation in the conflict in Syria, the NATO missile defense system being placed around Russia in violation of agreements made at the end of the cold war is reinstating a cold war with another nuclear power. The revolution and conflict in the Ukraine was instigated by a full court press by western elite associated the CFR. War hawk John McCain (CFR) appeared at a rally with the leader of the Ukrainian neo-Nazi Svoboda party leader. Need to ask yourself what the hell does representing Arizona as a congressman have to do with a revolution in Ukraine? Omidyar Network funded part of the Ukrainian protest movement. The Omidyar Network is the NGO of billionaire Ebay co-founder Pierre Omidyar. Also involved are organizations and money funded by George Soros (CFR).

If the shoe were on the other foot, what would the US response to Russian oligarchs causing problems in Mexico? How would we respond if that relationship was turned to be no longer favorable to our interests? Most worrying about the interference of the global elites are its potential implications. As Russia's every move is now being scrutinized for a possible military response to the ongoing crisis, the specter of a larger military operation now hangs over Eastern Europe.

As "mainstream media" outlets throw their support behind the CFR related billionaire oligarchs and NGOs that have helped to destabilize the country, and as neocons unite with neoliberals in their agenda to carve up Ukraine for western interests. All the while Joe Biden's (CFR) son, Hunter Biden and his fellow cronies Christopher Heinz (CFR) and Devon Archer are appointed to the Board of Ukraine's largest independent oil and gas company Burisma Holdings. Conflict of interest? Putin has railed against the western journalists for their "tall tales" in blindly repeating lies and misinformation provided to them by the United States on its anti-ballistic missile systems being constructed in Eastern Europe.

"We know year by year what's going to happen, and they know that we know. It's only you that they tell tall tales to, and you buy it, and spread it to the citizens of your countries. You people in turn do not feel a sense of the impending danger - this is what worries me. How do you not understand that the world is being pulled in an irreversible direction? While they pretend that nothing is going on. I don't know how to get through to you anymore." - Vladimir Putin

World War II

December 7th 1941, the Japanese Navy attacks the Pearl Harbor destroying or sinking 18 ships and killing over 2000 soldiers. This is the event the forced America into World War II. It was a day of tragedy. Congress declared war as a result, but the American public wanted to know why we were caught off guard. The Roberts

Commission was formed to investigate the attack. The Roberts Commission was headed by Owen Roberts, a Supreme Court Justice who was friendly with President Roosevelt. His commission found that everyone in Washington lived up to their obligations and duty, and the fault laid with the commanders in Hawaii.

Two commanders in Hawaii got blamed for not properly responding to the threat of attack, Admiral Husband Kimmel and General Walter C. Short. The media spread the story that it was because of their lack of oversight and dereliction of duty this horrible tragedy happened. They were flooded with hate mail, death threats, and people in Congress were calling for them to be shot.

Kimmel and Short fought the findings of the Roberts Commission report. Roberts was running a very unusual hearing. Evidence was being heard without being recorded. Statements were not made under oath. Both Kimmel and Short were denied to question witnesses or have other officers serve as council. The report omitted a significant amount of testimony. There is proof that FDR had foreknowledge, and people that were part of the CFR filled cabinet. The American public wasn't supposed to know the truth.

In 1944 the Army Peril Harbor board convened. The attorneys for Kimmel and Short provided proof that Washington had complete foreknowledge of the attack. They held this knowledge and did not pass it to the commanders in Hawaii. They found, "Up to the morning of December 7, 1941 everything that the Japanese were planning to do was known to the United States." FDR ordered the verdict to be classified. So how did Washington know of the attack beforehand? Pulitzer prize winning journalist John Toland, and World War II expert wrote about this extensively in his book *Infamy*. The US had broken the code Japan used for communication between its embassies and consulates. As a result, transcripts were given the same day to FDR, Army Chief of Staff George Marshall (CFR), and Secretary of State Cordell Hull (CFR). These messages indicated that they were planning on breaking relations with the US, and planning into entering War with the US. The Dutch Army intercepted a Japanese message forecasting an attack on Hawaii. The Dutch passed the message along to the US military observer in Java, Brigadier General Elliot Thorpe. Commander in the United States in the Dutch occupied Java. Thorp sent 4 messages to Washington of the impending attack, the War Department ordered him to send no further warnings... Another warning came in from Dusko Popov, a Yugoslavian double agent. Through contact with the Germans he learned of an impending attack on Pearl Harbor from the Japanese. He notified the FBI, and J. Edgar Hoover stated he passed the information on to FDR. It has been proven in his book *Day of Deceit: The Truth About FDR and Pearl Harbor*. Robert Stinnett obtained information through the Freedom of Information Act proves Washington had complete knowledge of the coming attack. Washington was deciphering both diplomatic and naval dispatch messages.

US public sentiment at the time was that they didn't want to get involved in another War. The suffering and pain of World War I was still an active memory in the collective psyche of the public. The elite knew they needed a galvanizing event to create outrage to draw the US into another War. This is the reason nothing was done to stop the attack in Pearl Harbor. This pattern of the Hegelian Dialectic is used over and over and over again. Common Sense and the Voice of Reason destroys the Hegelian Dialectic. When will we wake up?

"The liberty of a democracy is not safe if the people tolerated the growth of private power to a point where it becomes stronger than

the democratic state itself. That in its essence is fascism: ownership of government by an individual, by a group, or any controlling private power." Franklin D. Roosevelt

Ironic how he is describing exactly what he was involved with, and what has been happening the last 100 years.

Vietnam

To start the Vietnam War the officials in Washington used the Gulf of Tonkin incident as a reason to start the war. In 1964 Congress passed the Gulf of Tonkin Resolution. After two alleged attacks on US destroyers. The government and the media told us it was something that occurred, but in reality it did not. Why? They wanted to provoke us into war. The elite CFR controlled government went into propaganda mode telling us a story that was not true which ultimately cost the lives of countless people. Lying Lyndon Johnson was able to escalate the war to which he committed hundreds of thousands of troops. Johnson described the attack as an unprovoked attack on a routine patrol. Backing his play during this period of time was Robert McNamara (CFR) and others from the Council on Foreign Relations who filled his cabinet. Knowing it was a complete lie they scarified the lives of 60,000 young men.

Also during this period of time there were black ops going on in Laos. Laos is a tiny country neighboring Vietnam. The CIA saw that part of winning in Vietnam was making friends with Laos. Laos had strategic importance. The Vietnamese communist in the north had been using a route that ran through Laos to move troops, weapons, and supplies. The CIA was called in and ordered to take care of the problem. This makes sense on the surface. In the villages of northern Laos the CIA made contract with the tribes there. 30,000 of the men were paid, trained, and signed up to fight for the CIA.

The tribesmen were happy to fight for the CIA as long as they could keep farming their cash crop opium. For centuries opium and heroin have been produced in Laos. Not only did the CIA let them keep producing heroin, but they set up distribution to neighboring countries via airplane. One of the countries which was flooded with heroin was southern Vietnam. A huge amount of the heroin fell into the hands of troops fighting in Vietnam who had been demoralized by the absolutely insane Rules of Engagement.

"Let me introduce myself, I'm king heroin. Known to all is a destroyer of man. When I first came nobody knows. I came from a land where the poppy grows. I'm a world power and all knows that it's true. Use me once and you'll know it too. I capture men's will and destroy their minds and cause them commit all sorts of crimes. In cellophane bags I found my way to great men in offices to children at play. From the riches of states to the poorest of slums. From the highest exalted to Bellary bums." –George Kirby Comedian

At present time, we need to ask ourselves what is going with the opiate epidemic in the country. We need to ask ourselves, why is the DEA trying to ban an herb called Kratom which has helped thousands kick opiate addiction? Why are they wanting to classify an herb as a Schedule I drug? Could it be big pharma owns the DEA, and a plant based remedy doesn't make them money? Opiates for a couple centuries have been used by the "elite" of society to soften up populations because of the destructive nature of its addiction. Jailing this people won't work, it will only further pull down society because of the social ripple effect that will carry on multigenerationally. We have created a cluster-fuck of epic proportions, but keep beating the iodic drum of the war on drugs. Maybe instead of going to war against your own people under the camouflage of drugs you help them so the ripple effect of societal destruction is hampered. So fucking stupid!

The American public by and large were unaware of the restrictions placed on the troops during the Vietnam War. Had they understood the restrictions imposed on our forces were so clearly unreasonable and immoral the American public would have been totally outraged. Therefore, the Rules of Engagement were classified until 1985. Senator Barry Goldwater who succeeded in their declassification said:

"These layers of restrictions, which were constantly changing and were almost impossible to memorize or understand, although it was required of our pilots, granted huge sanctuary areas to the enemy. When certain limits would at last be removed after repeated appeals by the Joint Chiefs, the reductions were made only in gradual steps and seldom were strong enough to serve our strategic ends. Numerous partial and total bombing halts interrupted the effectiveness of earlier bombing campaigns. Often, when limited extensions of target areas were granted, they were unexpectedly canceled and withdrawn shortly afterward. What were some of the rules?"

It didn't get much better for the ground troops. Ground assaults in urban areas known to shelter enemy forces generally had to be preceded by loud-speaker warnings and leaflet drops. This is forecasting to the enemy. This is like telling the defensive team your play before the ball is snapped in a football game. Our troops could return fire only when the enemy was positively identified and in close contact. Sniper and mortar fire were not counted as contact unless such fire interferes with the scheme of maneuver or is inflicting casualties or damage to equipment. Never mind, you are having live ammo shot at you. Only flat-trajectory weapons (rifles, machine guns, grenades and recoilless rifles) could be used in civilian-populated areas, which largely exposed our men, and then only if there was a specific, identifiable target. These guys where put through a meat grinder when this war could have been easily one in short order. You see how that works folks, they don't give a flying fuck about you. It's all lip service. They treated these young men as cannon fodder.

This tragic episode was run almost entirely by CFR members. William P. Bundy (CFR) drafted the Tonkin Gulf Resolution before the now-discredited Tonkin Gulf Incident even took place. Bundy's father-in-law, Dean Acheson (CFR), as leader of a senior team of advisers nicknamed "the Wise Men," persuaded Lyndon Baines Johnson to dramatically escalate the war beginning in 1965. And Secretary of Defense Robert McNamara (CFR) helped develop the Rules of Engagement. How were these CFR member punished for causing needless death and suffering of Americans? Bundy was rewarded when he left the State Department. David Rockefeller (CFR) appointed him editor of the CFR's journal Foreign Affairs. McNamara, one of the leading architects of the Vietnam War debacle, became president of the World Bank.

Who was benefiting from purposely dragging this war out so long? Not the American public, certainly not the Vietnamese, only banking interests and military industrial war complex.

Operation Northwoods

On March 13, 1962, the Joints Chiefs of Staff proposed to President F. Kennedy that the US should attack itself and blame Cuba to provoke outrage for war. Northwoods was a Joint Chiefs of Staff response to a request from Edward Lansdale (CFR). This document described pretexts which could be created to provoke war and was signed by Joint Chief of Staff Chief Lyman Lemnitzer (CFR) and sent to Secretary of Defense Robert McNamara (CFR). "We could develop a Communist Cuban terror campaign in the Miami area, in other Florida cities and even in Washington. The terror campaign could be pointed at refugees seeking haven in the United States. We could sink a boatload of Cubans en route to Florida (real or simulated). We could foster attempts on lives of Cuban refugees in the United States even to the extent of wounding in instances to be widely publicized. Exploding a few plastic bombs in carefully chosen spots, the arrest of Cuban agents and the release of prepared documents substantiating Cuban involvement, also would be helpful in projecting the idea of an irresponsible government."

Other ideas were discussed such as calling for innocent people to be shot on American streets; and hijacking planes. Using phony evidence, all of it would be blamed on Castro, thus giving Lemnitzer and his CFR buddies the excuse they needed to launch their war. The operation was rejected by John F Kennedy for grounds of being completely immoral.

Today

During his campaign, Obama selected the Zbigniew Brzezinski (CFR), as one of his top advisors. Obama called Brzezinski "one of our more outstanding thinkers" and "somebody I have learned an immense amount from." Presumably Brzezinski's teachings included the world government he advocates.

"Major world powers, new and old, also face a novel reality: while the lethality of their military might be greater than ever, their capacity to impose control over the <u>politically awakened masses</u> of the world is at a historic low... To put it bluntly: in earlier times, it
209

was easier to control one million people than to physically kill one million people; today, it is infinitely easier to kill one million people than to control one million people." –Zbigniew Brzezinksi, Speech on 9/17/2008 Chatham House London.

For Treasury Secretary, Obama chose Timothy Geithner: Senior Fellow in International Economics at the CFR, Bilderberger, former head of the New York Federal Reserve, and former employee of both the IMF and Kissinger Associates. That is balls deep in the establishment. Geithner managed the bailout of Wall Street with taxpayer dollars. Assisting Geithner at the Treasury in overseeing the auto industry bailout is fellow CFR member Stephen Rattner.

Director of the National Economic Council, a U.S. government agency created by a Bill Clinton executive order, Obama selected Lawrence Summers (CFR, Bilderberger). Henry Kissinger (CFR) had said Summers should "be given a White House post in which he was charged with shooting down or fixing bad ideas."

Defense Secretary, Obama elected to continue with Bush's choice of Robert Gates (CFR, Bilderberger). During the Carter administration, Gates served as a special assistant to Zbigniew Brzezinski (CFR, co-founder Trilateral Commission). In 2004, he co-chaired a CFR Task Force on Iran with Brzezinski, who lauded Gates in Time in 2008. Joining Gates in the Defense Department are fellow CFR members Michele Flournoy (Under Secretary of Defense for Policy), Jeh C. Johnson (Defense Department General Counsel), and Kathleen Hicks (Deputy Under Secretary of Defense for Strategy, Plans and Forces).

Obama chose Hillary Clinton as Secretary of State, who has attended the top-secret Bilderberger meetings. Hillary is not a CFR member, but husband Bill is member of the Trilateral Commission.

Her State Department was packed with CFR members, including James B. Steinberg (Deputy Secretary of State), William J. Burns (Under Secretary for Political Affairs), Susan Rice (U.S. Ambassador to the UN), Jacob J. Lew (Deputy Secretary of State for Management and Resources), Todd Stern (Special Envoy for Climate Change), and many others. Here's Hillary talking about her and the State Department's relationship with the Council on Foreign Relations.

"Thank you very much, Richard, and I am delighted to be here in these new headquarters. I have been often to, I guess, the 'mother ship' in New York City, but it's good to have an outpost of the Council right here down the street from the State Department. We get a lot of advice from the Council, so this will mean I won't have as far to go to be told what we should be doing." –Hillary Clinton, US Secretary of State

The Orwellian surveillance society of the Department of Homeland Security was conceived before 9/11 by a task force called the U.S. Commission on National Security. Nine of the 12 members belonged to the CFR. The administration of the department under Obama has been heavily staffed with CFR members since its inspection. Including Janet Napolitano (Secretary), Jane Holl Lute (Deputy Secretary), Juliette Kayyem (Assistant Secretary, Office of Intergovernmental Programs), and Alan Bersin (Assistant Secretary, Office of International Affairs).

As long as the CFR and big money interests control our government, we can anticipate more of the same. There will be no changes. Expect more: diminishing national sovereignty; free flow of immigration; increasing jobs losses through multinational trade agreements like the NAFTA and TPP; further internationalization of law; increasing loss of freedoms in a "surveillance society";

211

progressive organization of the United States, Mexico, and Canada into a North American Union; climate change plans that do not address the problem, but create policy to usurp control and ultimately, broader merger into a world government where all power will be concentrated in the hands of the elite. All it takes for this inertia to continue is ignorant people believing their leaders' lies and apathy for this nightmare to be realized.

In a WiliLeaks email dated 3/13/2016 from Bill Ivey to Washington insider and Hillary Clinton Champaign manager John Podesta describes the state of the molding of an ignorant electorate as they battle to get Hillary elected over Trump. Ivey, appointed Chairman of the National Endowment for the Arts by Bill Clinton, a trustee of the Center of American Progress, and a team leader in the Obama presidential transition was writing Podesta concerned about the reality star power of Trump. He also went on to say the following. "And as I've mentioned, we've all been quite content to demean government, drop civics and in general conspire to produce an unaware and compliant citizenry. The unawareness remains strong but compliance is obviously fading rapidly. This problem demands some serious, serious thinking — and not just poll driven, demographically-inspired messaging." Here is just another example of another the startling admission to manipulate the masses and short circuit democracy.

"One of the penalties for refusing to participate in politics is that you end up being governed by you inferiors." - Plato

Science of Control

There is a scientific way to verify what's really going on if history and current events seem too spooky, or the cognitive dissonance of having to change your thoughts is too strong. It's the emerging field of science called the Science of Complexity. It is the study of complex systems, systems with many parts that interact to produce global behavior that cannot easily be explained in terms of interactions between the individual constituent elements. Rule interactions and how it relates to its network in complex systems emerges. Examples of complex systems networks are in Biology, Physics, and computer science. Until recently, economics was ignored because it was pretty much guided by ideology rather than scientific data. Three complex systems theorist at the Swiss Federal Institute of Technology in Zurich conducted a study empirically identify a network of power. This study combined mathematics used in natural system with comprehensive corporate data to map ownership among the world's largest multinational, dubbed The *Network of Global Corporate Control.*

This database was comprised of 37 million companies and investors from all over the world. They identified the largest 43,060 of them and the share ownership linking them. From there they constructed a model of which companies controlled others through shareholding networks, and revenue.

What emerged was a power structure. One of the study's authors remarked, "Reality is complex, we must move away from dogma, whether it's conspiracy theories or free-market." When the team worked through the information and relationships much of the ownership tracked back to a "super-entity" of 147 companies. "In effect, less than 1 per cent of the companies were able to control 40 per cent of the entire network," says Glattfelder. Most were financial institutions. The top 20 included Barclays Bank, JPMorgan Chase & Co, and The Goldman Sachs Group. Of course they are financial institutions, when you can make money out of nothing you get to control the game. Acquiring holdings in companies that actually produce useful goods is rather easy.

Most of these companies are members of the Council on Foreign relations or their counter parts in other countries. This should come at no great surprise that if you have the ability to make and control money you get to buy everything of real value. What is so shocking is how people cannon understand this simple concept, or understand its implications. If you gave my 8 year old the power to make and control money, he could put 2 and 2 together pretty quickly to figure out he could buy anything he wanted. On the macro level, it's not much more complicated than that folks. Any arguments to the contrary are bullshit, lies or economic ideological dribble. The proof is in the pudding of this study, and crazy wealth inequality we are experiencing. How this simple fact of our reality flies below the radar of the American public without causing outrage is beyond me. But, we understand how it got that way.

"Until the control of the issue of currency and credit is restored to government and recognized as its most conspicuous and sacred responsibility, all talks of sovereignty of Parliament and of democracy is idle and futile." -William Lyon Mackenzie King, Prime Minister of Canada 1921-1926.

Membership

The list of the CFR members comprises the most powerful and influential in the country. Depending on your ideology you'll find both, your hero's and your sworn enemies. Let's take a look at the current administration and the last two to get an idea of the influence of this group. This lists is not exhaustive, but informational.

Bill Clinton Administration - He is a member of the CFR and Trilateral Commission.

Albert Gore, Jr. (Vice-President)

Donna E. Shalala (Secretary of Health and Human Services)

Laura D. Tyson (Chairman of the Council of Economic Advisors)

Alice M Rivlin (Deputy Director of the Office of Management and Budget)

Madeline K. Albright (U.S. Ambassador to the U.N.)

Warren Christopher (Secretary of State)

Clifton R. Wharton, Jr. (Deputy Secretary of State and former Chairman of the Rockefeller Foundation)

Les Aspin (Secretary of Defense)

Colin Powell (Chairman, Joint Chiefs of Staff)

W. Anthony Lake (National Security Advisor)

George Stephanopoulos (Senior Advisor)

Samuel R. 'Sandy' Berger (Deputy National Security Advisor)

R. James Woolsey (CIA Director)

William J. Crowe, Jr. (Chairman of the Foreign Intelligence Advisory Board)

Lloyd Bentsen (former member, Secretary of Treasury)

Roger C. Altman (Deputy Secretary of Treasury)

Henry G. Cisneros (Secretary of Housing and Urban Development)

Bruce Babbit (Secretary of the Interior)

Peter Tarnoff (Under Secretary of State for International Security of Affairs)

Winston Lord (Assistant Secretary of State for East Asian and Pacific Affairs)

Strobe Talbott (Aid Coordinator to the Commonwealth of Independent States)

Alan Greenspan (Chairman of the Federal Reserve System)

Walter Mondale (U.S. Ambassador to Japan)

Ronald H. Brown (Secretary of Commerce)

Franklin D. Raines (Economics and International Trade).

George W. Bush Administration - He is not a member of the CFR, however his father is a member.

Richard Cheney (Vice President,)

Colin Powell (Secretary of State)

Condoleeza Rice (National Security Advisor)

Robert B. Zoellick (U.S. Trade Representative)

Elaine Chao (Secretary of Labor)

Brent Scowcroft (Chairman of the Foreign Intelligence Advisory Board)

Richard Haass (Director of Policy Planning at the State Dept. and Ambassador at Large)

Henry Kissinger (Pentagon Defense Policy Board)

Robert Blackwill (U.S. Ambassador to Indial)

Stephen Friedman (Sr. White House Economic Advisor)

Stephen Hadley (Deputy National Security Advisor)

Richard Perle (Chairman of Pentagon Defense Policy Board)

Paul Wolfowitz (Assistant Secretary of Defense)

Dov S. Zakheim (Under Secretary of Defense, Comptroller)

I. Lewis Libby (Chief of Staff for the Vice President).

Barack Obama Administration - Not a member, but highly connected to CFR. During his campaign he had the following CFR members has his adviors: Zbigniew Bzrezinshi, Anthony Lake, Eric Schwartz, Lawrence Korb, Madeleine Albright, William Daley, Bruce Reidel, and Daniel Tarullo.

Timothy Geithner (Secretary of Treasury)

George Mitchell (Middle East Envoy)

Richard Holbrooke (Special Envoy)

David Cohen (Special Envoy)

Robert Gates (Secretary of Defense) ,

Admiral Dennis Blair (Director of National Intelligence)

Sanjay Gupta (Surgeon General)

Susan Rice (Ambassador to the United Nations)

Ivo Daalder (National Security Council member)

Dennis Ross (State Department Special Envoy)

Kurt M. Campbell (Assistant Secretary of State for East Asian and Pacific Affairs)

Louis Caldera (James Steinberg White House Military Office)

James L. Jones (National Security Advisor General)

Richard Haas (State Department Special Envoy)

Thomas Donilon (Deputy National Security Advisor)

Stephen Flynn (Policy National Security Working Group -member)

Eric Shinseki (Secretary of Veterans Affairs)

Paul Volke(Chairman of the Economic Recovery Committee)

The Merging of Money, Politics, and Media into Power

Globalists like George Soros to people who own the news media such as Rupert Murdoch are all part of this Group. The most rich and powerful companies are tied to the organization along with their owners. It's an orgy of power consisting of: finance, politics, military, intelligence, media, education, medicine, labor unions, and food. People associated to this group are in control of every aspect of life and they answer to nobody. The politicians are put in place to take blame for the societal ills caused by these people, and give you an illusion of choice. The world model that benefits these people is neoliberal free market corporate globalization with a healthy dose of propaganda and lack of transparency. They promote powerful coercive activist state for the capitalist ruling class which is lorded over the rest of us. In other words, two sets of rules. It forces its agenda globally via military and economic forces when there is no benefit for the common people except for perceived feelings of safety and righteous indignation which for the most part was fostered from lies in the news media. The media is used as a system for pushing their agenda. Why no 3rd party or independents get relatively no coverage? The canned answer is why bother knowing what they have to say, there not going to win anyway. Buy <u>why</u>? The MAIN reason they are not going to win is because nobody knows who the fuck they are because the media refuses to cover them on purpose! They are in the pocket of the corporate elite. If this was a free society with a free press, voice would be given to these people's ideas instead of wasting it on horseshit stories and celebrity news. No wonder confidence in the media is at an all-time low. People are tired of being lied to. A 2014 Gallup Poll rated news confidence rating was 22%. How much worse does our news have to get before we are knocking on the door of Soviet Russia or North Korea for accuracy in reporting. It's time to wake the fuck up and start asking questions.

A perfect example is the mess in Syria. We have been fed a narrative that we are helping the people of Syria by arming the moderate rebels. The US has been backing radicals to over through the government via the CIA. Our tax dollars and going to arm these people halfway a world away, for what purpose? After our involvement decimates this area of the world, it causes a migration crisis in Europe resulting in a cultural war and untold human suffering. What these idiots don't mention is that when you fuck with people, kill family, and destroy their homes that tends to make more terrorists. Meanwhile, a company called Genie Energy is drilling in Golan Heights, a portion of Syria annexed by Israel during the conflict Syria has been experiencing. Golan Heights is a very rich oil field. Controlling members of Genie Energy are Rupert Murdoch, Dick Cheney, and Jacob Rothschild. You can't make this shit up, this is a "conspiracy theorist" wet dream. The CFR agenda has been to overthrow the Assad government, then you have CFR members profiting off the mess their policies have caused. Notice Genie Energy been talked about in the news? Yeah, not much. I guess they don't want that genie out of the bottle. Could it have anything to do with the fact Rupert Murdoch owns a huge percentage of the news? Dick Cheney war profiteering again? Jacob Rothschild profiting following in his generations old family footsteps and profiting off war and human suffering again? The company where Cheney was CEO before being Bush's VP, Halliburton received a no-bid contract to rebuild Iraq after we started a war under false pretenses. There is also not very much talk about the roll of pipeline that would cut through Syria which is central issue to the war. The problem is the narrative we are receiving is not based in reality. This is only a couple examples.

The mass media does not report facts, they report narratives to mold the thoughts of the populous. The real power brokers use the threat of terrorism to do whatever they want around the world. However, underlying all this death are people profiting. People in the highest positions of business and government make a shit ton of money convincing us of terrorist threats which they created. They expect us to put our kids' lives on the line without complete information or information that turns out to be lies. Such as going into Iraq without ever being held accountable. From all this death they are able to make huge profits from the military industrial complex which is being funded by our tax dollars to which we are held as collateral. We, the American public, are experiencing the collateral economic damage of such decision making. Then they go into these areas and exploit the natural resources. Dick Cheney is a living example of this phenomenon along with a lot people that are part of the Council on Foreign Relations. Look into them, see how they have gone in and out of government and big business which deals with the most critical parts of our society. They are holding the levers of society. So when we bitch about society being fucked up, CFR and its' connected groups is where we should be looking. Look past the puppets and see their puppeteers.

"Main function of the military, or the National Institutes of Health, or the rest of the federal system, is to provide some device to socialize costs, get the public to pay the costs, to take the risks. Ultimately, if anything comes out, you put it into private pockets. And, again, this has to be done in a way that protects state power and private power from the domestic enemy. You have to say it's to defend ourselves against Grenada or Russia or Guatemala or somebody. If you get people frightened enough, they won't notice that their taxes are going into creating the profits of IBM and Merck twenty years from now. Why not tell them the truth? Because then they might not make these decisions." -Noam Chomsky

Here's a list of some of the companies which comprise the list of companies which are part of the CFR. Energy, banking, media, food production, etc. are all rolled into this group. The power the CFR is the most unrecognized power in society. It's a pretty long list.

• ABC News

•Alcoa

•American Express

•AIG

- Bank of America
- Bloomberg
- Boeing
- BP
- Chevron
- Citigroup
- Coca Cola
- De Beers
- Deutsche Bank
- ExxonMobil
- FedEx
- Ford Motor
- General Electric
- GlaxoSmithKline
- Google
- Goldman Sachs
- Halliburton

It's a long list, it keeps going for a while as you can tell. Comprising of most of the powerful companies.

•Heinz

•Hess

•IBM•JP Morgan Chase

•Kohlberg Kravis Roberts & Co.

•Lehman Brothers

•Lockheed Martin

•MasterCard

•McGraw-Hill

•McKinsey

•Merck

•Merrill Lynch

•Motorola

•Nasdaq

•News Corp

•Nike

•Pepsi

•Pfizer

•Shell Oil

•Sony Corporation of America

•Tata Group

•Time Warner

- Total S.A.
- Toyota Motor North America
- UBS
- United Technologies
- United States Chamber of Commerce
- U.S. Trust Corporation
- Verizon
- Visa

Notable Quotables?

As always quoting out of context is problematic. However, some quotes from notable people who have been part of the close to or part of the establishment should be illuminating.

"The real truth of the matter is, as you and I know, that a financial element in the large centers has owned the government of the U.S. since the days of Andrew Jackson." - Franklin D. Roosevelt

"I am a most unhappy man. I have unwillingly ruined my country. A great industrial nation is controlled by its system of credit. Our system of credit is concentrated in the hands of a few men." - Woodrow Wilson

"We have restricted credit, we have restricted opportunity, we have controlled development, and we have come to be one of the worst ruled, one of the most completely controlled and dominated governments in the world... no longer a government of free opinion, no longer a government by conviction and a vote of the majority, but

a government by the opinion and duress of small groups of dominant men." - Woodrow Wilson

"The high office of President has been used to foment a plot to destroy the American's freedom, and before I leave office I must inform the citizen of his plight." -John F. Kennedy, ten days before he was assassinated.

"If we understand the mechanism and motives of the group mind, it is now possible to control and regiment the masses according to our will without them knowing it." - Edward Bernays, father of public relations and propaganda.

"The individual is handicapped by coming face to face with a conspiracy so monstrous he cannot believe it exists." - J. Edgar Hoover

"The drive of the Rockefellers and their allies is to create a one-world government combining super capitalism and Communism under the same tent, all under their control. Do I mean conspiracy? Yes I do. I am convinced there is such a plot, international in scope, generations old in planning, and incredibly evil in intent." Congressman Larry P. McDonald

"This conjunction of an immense military establishment and large arms industry is new in the American Experience... We recognize the imperative need for this development. Yet we must not fail to comprehend its grave implications... In the councils of government, we must guard against the acquisition of unwarranted influence, whether sought or unsought, by the military-industrial complex. The potential for the disastrous rise of misplaced power exists and will persist. -Dwight D. Eisenhower

"We are grateful to the Washington Post, The New York Times, Time Magazine and other great publication whose directors have attended

our meetings and respected their promises of discretion for almost forty years. It would have been impossible for us to develop our plan for the world if we had been subject to the bright lights of publicity during those years. But, the work is now much more sophisticated and prepare to march towards a world government. The supranational sovereignty of an intellectual elite and world bankers is surely preferable to the national auto determination practiced in past centuries." David Rockefeller former chairman of the CFR.

"It's good to be back at the Council on Foreign Relations... I have been a member for a long time and was actually a director for some period of time. I never mentioned that when I was campaigning for re-election back home in Wyoming." -Dick Cheney

If we want real change we need to identify people associated to this center of power, and recognize the reality of the world we live in. We need to understand we are being led by people who do not give a shit about the wellbeing of the American public. We have been used as the force to propagate their ambitions at our expense.

Straight from the Horse's Mouth.

These are quotes from the President of the CFR, Richard N. Haass, relating to Sovereignty and Globalization. One thing is clear, the model of capitalism we are experiencing neoliberalism is a result of decision making

"The near monopoly of power once enjoyed by sovereign entities is being eroded. As a result, new mechanisms are needed for regional and global governance that include actors other than states. This is not to argue that Microsoft, Amnesty International, or Goldman Sachs be given seats in the United Nations General Assembly, but it does mean including representatives of such organizations in

regional and global deliberations when they have the capacity to affect whether and how regional and global challenges are met. Moreover, states must be prepared to cede some sovereignty to world bodies if the international system is to function."

"Globalization thus implies that sovereignty is not only becoming weaker in reality, but that it needs to become weaker. States would be wise to weaken sovereignty in order to protect themselves, because they cannot insulate themselves from what goes on elsewhere. Sovereignty is no longer a sanctuary."

"Necessity may also lead to reducing or even eliminating sovereignty when a government, whether from a lack of capacity or conscious policy, is unable to provide for the basic needs of its citizens. This reflects not simply scruples, but a view that state failure and genocide can lead to destabilizing refugee flows and create openings for terrorists to take root."

"The goal should be to redefine sovereignty for the era of globalization, to find a balance between a world of fully sovereign states and an international system of either world government or anarchy."

The Two Party System

The two party system is bankrolled by the people in control give no voice to the American Public. As illustrated earlier, this has been happening for over 100 years. Results of this arrangement cannot get any clearer when nobody is happy with what the government does. These guys have been working for the same power brokers of this country for decades. There is no party that represents the normal person. It really doesn't matter what is said during elections. It's what's done, and how that results culminate

227

into our present day situation. In 2016, Obama said, "Democracy works, this country works when you have two parties that are serious and trying to solve problems." It's working for who? Talk is cheap when it doesn't match actions. Talk is only worth something when it is coherent with action. They seem to make more problems than they solve. Thinking people who care need form their own movement independent of big money, and abandon the people who do not have our best interest at heart regardless of party Republican or Democrat. On an appearance of the Conan O'Brian show illustrated the ridiculousness of it all when Bill Burr was asked if he watched the convention.

"No, I think if you watch those you're an idiot. I don't understand why you would sit there wasting your time when they are all saying the same thing. Like, you know over the last four years everything good that happened was cause of us and we would have done more good stuff if it wasn't for those guys. Then the democrats say no we did all the good stuff. It's like you are all working for the same guy. They have been on both horses and it just kind of goes. It's not for you. You vote for the guy that says there is like a meteor headed right toward the planet. That's the guy you vote for. Yeah, the psycho you know there for sure isn't any corporate money behind that guy. That guy is going to come on TV he's going to be reading files from the Pentagon. You know what they're doing, you know what else they are doing. Just freaking people out. As unsettling as that is you could at least believe him, trust him. I think the republicans and democrats just say the same things and wait for applause breaks. I think it's time to get this country back to work and everyone cheers."
Bill Burr

Bill Burr is making a valid point in his comedy. A leader who isn't backed by corporate interests that is transparent with the citizens would blow peoples' minds. In fact, democracy is built upon the founding principles of transparency and an informed public. It's hard to have a successful society when is bought and sold and we are treated like chattel. The public is being continually misinformed by both parties. At this point our best option is to inform others of this fraud, collectively create some goals based off human decency which will fundamentally shift power back to the people. That shift will not come from anyone associated with the CFR, Trilateral commission or high in finance. This shift will have to be grass-roots organization of people who are fed up, based upon common sense, human values, and not ideologically driven. Or we can continue living in the fantasy hell.

"The world of politics is actually without gender or color. It is incredibly honest band non-judgmental. The color is white, the color

is green. The color of the dollar. It doesn't matter who you vote for. If you want a change, if you want your country back, if you want to go on a journey that helps lesbians and colored people and people looking for jobs and retiring and all sorts of different people, you have to get involved in politics. Stop trusting politicians to do it for you because they are not going to do it. They don't work for you, they work for big business." – Russell Brand

Moving Forward?

First thing is first, smash political ideologies. Topics that promote individual freedom are universal and stand up to ridicule no matter the source. Understand fear has been, and always will be used by people in power to cast authority over and influence others. Recognize that fear propagated by people in power almost always comes in forms of incomplete narratives.

Descriptions are not explanations. The main reason for the copious amounts of classified documents is not to keep us safe, it's to keep the empire builders safe from us, and to deny us proper explanations. Identify the problem makers. The Council of Foreign Relations and its ilk need to be brought to their knees for crimes against the American public. For pushing US foreign policy into a costly death march of globalization. With few exceptions most establishment Republicans and Democrat in high positions can't be trusted. Have an honest moment with yourself and ask who trusts either Bush presidents, the Clintons, or Obama? They've all had a turn screwing over the middle class. They need to be held accountable for the debt bondage system that has been created, and they continue to propagate. This group of policy making Washington DC leeches have been using the American public for the last 100 years. Think about it, out of 300 million people in the US and all we get is shit for leaders. The reason is they are not working for us! They work for the people who are the real owners and they are power hungry.

"I canon accept, your canon that we are to judge pope and king unlike other men, with a favorable presumption that they do no wrong. If there is any presumption, it is the other way agains the holders of power... Power tends to corrupt, and absolute power corrupts absolutely." Lord Dalberg-Acton

There is a reason for this corruption of power, and it's rooted in our biology. This is the underlying reason why separation of powers and why a free objective press is important to a free society. It's a safety mechanism that keeps those in power from engorging themselves on the sovereignty of others within a free society to benefit themselves. This has been side stepped in our society.

Power changes the brain, triggering increased testosterone in both men and women. Testosterone and one of its by-products called 3-androstanediol, are addictive, largely because they increase dopamine in a part of the brain's reward system called the nucleus accumbens. Cocaine effects the same system. It even works the same in our primate cousins the baboons. Baboons lower in the hierarchy have lower levels of dopamine in key brain areas, but if they get "promoted" to a higher position in ape society, then dopamine rises.

This makes them more aggressive and sexually active. In humans similar changes happen when people are given power.

Bill Clinton and Donald Trump are perfect example of this biology, they are acting like apes, allegedly. Same with a lot of rich and powerful men, they have a hard time keeping their dick where it should belong. Think about all the political and big executive sex scandals, this is rooted in biology. The only way to fight this

231

problem is being mindful of this biological interaction. Dopamine improves the functioning of the brain's frontal lobes.

Conversely, demotion in a hierarchy decreases dopamine levels, increases stress and reduces cognitive function. We see this being manifest when under privileged groups are rioting, but their angst is miss directed to anything other than the source of their troubles. Isn't it ironic how people like George Soros and his ilk are the ones funding groups such as BLM, but are the ones that are controlling the mechanisms which are causing the harm in the first place? Puppet mastery at its worst. Too much power can equal too much dopamine which disrupts normal cognition and emotion. Leading to gross errors of judgment and imperviousness to risk, not to mention huge egocentricity and lack of empathy for others. This is part of the reason pretty much all dictators and people with too much power are bat-shit crazy. Imagine being born into this world of the elite, your world view is completely different than the common person.

Start researching historical topics and follow the money. Why is the money trail never followed in the mass murder known as war, but always followed in any other crime? It's simply because the narrative you've been fed by the news media and school would get turned on its head. What's the difference between people in a government scheming together to kill the enemy or the mob doing a hit? Morally there is no difference, except the public accepts one version as being acceptable. Question everything, if it doesn't make sense keep questioning, and never accept bullshit. The one thing these people do not want is a public awaking to how badly we have been getting screwed. In 2012, Zbigniew Brzezinski's (CFR) call of warning to the "global political awakening" has only intensified in recent years. During a speech in Poland, Brzezinski noted that it has become "increasingly difficult to suppress" and control the "persistent and highly motivated populist resistance of politically awakened and historically resentful peoples." Brzezinski also blamed the accessibility of "radio, television and the Internet" for the "universal awakening of mass political consciousness."

The political spectrum as understood; far left is Communism and far right is Fascism as opposites on a spectrum is complete horseshit. Effectively they are the same. Here is the real spectrum: Happy way of life vs an exploited way of life. The more centralized power in government becomes the more tyrannical it will become. The more dispersed the power of government among the citizenry the more free a society becomes. There has never been one government in the modern world with centralized power that has not been oppressive to its people. It always goes hand-in-hand, and cannot be separated. It's like saying the color black is not dark.

Remember the word government comes from two Latin words.

Gubernare: to control, rule, guide, govern.

Mente: mind

Government literally means mind control. It makes perfect sense, the government is crazy and so is what is happening in this country. Wake up, think for yourself, tap into the curiosity you had as a kid, and use the voice of reason to find truth. Common Sense is the only thing that will get us out of this cluster fuck.

If you want change, it will only happen if you get informed.

In the information age, we have the world's knowledge at our finger tips. Be your own detective and empower yourself with knowledge in trying to find answers. There has been a lot written on the topic of the Council on Foreign Relations. Some good, some inaccurate, but after considerable research an informational mosaic takes shape of the real power structure of this county. Below are some suggestions if you want more background on the troubles we are facing. The troubles won't go away until we recognize the problems and make them go away. Research what these authors are talking about. All of them have content independent of the books they have written, and can be looked up online. There are also some great websites out there that provide historically accurate content and thought provoking discussion.

Gilens, Martin & Page Benjamin. *Testing Theories of American Politics: Elites, Interest Groups, and Average Citizens.* American Political Science Association. 2014

> *This is a Princeton University study that was conducted and came to the conclusion that the US is no longer a democracy, but in effect functions as an oligarchy. "The central Point that emerges from our research is that economic elites and organized groups representing business interests have substantial independent impacts on US government policy, while mass-based interest groups and average citizens have little or no independent influence."*

Quigley, Carroll. *Tragedy and Hope.* GSG and Associates. 2004.

> *"This massive hardcover book of 1348 pages provides a detailed world history beginning with the industrial revolution and imperialism through two world wars, a global depression and the rise of communism. Tragedy & Hope is the definitive work on the world's power structure and an essential source material for understanding the history, goals and actions of the elite."*

Quigley, Carroll. *The Anglo American Establishment.* Gsg & Assoc. 1981.

> *"Quigley exposes the secret societies established in London in 1891, by Cecil Rhodes. Quigley explains how these men worked in union to begin their society to control the world. He explains how all the wars from that time were deliberately created to control the economies of all the*

nations. Carroll Quigley (1910-1977) was a highly respected professor at the School of Foreign Service at Gerogetown University. He was an instructor at Princeton and Harvard; a consultant to the U.S. Department of Defense, the House Committee on Astronautics and Space Exploration; and the U.S. Navy."

Plummer, Joseph. *Tragedy and Hope 101, The Illusion of Justice, Freedom, and Democracy.* Brushfire Publishing. 2014.

"Based on the groundbreaking research of respected historian Carroll Quigley, Tragedy and Hope 101 reveals an unimaginably devious political system, skillfully manipulated by a handful of elite, which is undermining freedom and democracy as we know it. The goal of those who control the system, in Quigley's own words, is to dominate "all habitable portions of the world." Using deception, theft, and violence, they have achieved more toward this goal than any rulers in human history." The material presented here is largely a matter of public record, with admittedly some speculation, which is unavoidable at certain points due to the secretive nature and power of the individuals and groups under investigation. The author, however, speculates on solid ground, informed by verifiable, historical facts that have been revealed by some of the very people who form what he calls "The Network."

Sutton, Antony. *Wall Street and the Bolshevik Revolution.* Arlington House. 1974.

Simpson, Colin. *Lusitania.* Prentice Hall Press. 1972

Zinn, Howard. *A People's History of the United States.* Harper & Row. 1980.

Stinnett, Robert. *Day of Deceit, The Truth About FDR and Pearl Harbor.* Free Press, Edition: Touchstone ed. 1999.

Butler, Major General Smedly. *War is a Racket.* Round Table Press. 1935.

Loewen, James. *Lies My Teacher Told Me: Everything Your American History Textbook Got Wrong.* Touchstone. 2007.

Some other resources to research which provides alternative perspectives:

Owned & Operated 2012 Documentary

www.theempirefiles.tv Empire Files: Abby Martin.

www.truthdig.com drilling beneath the headlines. A Progressive Journal of News and Opinion.

Chapter 7

Solutions

"Sometimes it falls upon a generation to be great, you can be that generation." – Nelson Mandela

To put it simply, we need a revolution of sorts. Not necessarily a forcible overthrow of government or social order for a new system, but an evolution which disempowers the old system of "elite" control. It's already happening in America, Asia, and South America as people start to wake up. Things don't get this bad and crazy without purposeful disregard of the citizens. It's time to recognize our trust has been misplaced, and it's time to throw out the scoundrels.

This is an evolution that is very badly needed in today society. We have a choice at this point in history. We keep going down the same path, with the same kind of collective thinking, and collapse back into ourselves like we have done before time after time throughout history. That's some real "children of the corn" shit. Or we use our highly evolved minds to become something completely better. Regardless of how badly we want to deny reality, play video games, fight with each other over petty shit, and get drunk we are all on this organic spherical spaceship called Earth hurtling through space at 1000 miles per hour. We know of the growing threat of global warming, pollution, and how banking and big business is exploiting us and the natural the resources. We see how this only empowers a very small minority. We need to turn things around, there must be an evolution in human thinking.

"There is one thing stronger than all the armies in the world, and that is the idea whose time has come." –Victor Hugo

Change is not impossible! In 1776, the founders of this country understood what freedom meant. Regardless of their short comings or racism, they had an ideal of freedom that still applies today to all men. They threw off the chains of British control when that seemed impossible. Britain was the most powerful empire in the world at the time. It doesn't matter black, white, Mexican or Jew we have been born with unalienable rights; that among these are life, liberty, and the pursuit of happiness.

Over the past 100 years our rights have been slowly eroded. How many of us can say we truly feel free? How many of us are truly happy with the current state of things? How many of us honestly believe the world in its current direction is going to be a better place for our children or grandchildren? We are entitled with the right to pursue happiness. We should be free people leaving lives of purpose which are not plagued by an out of control prison population, drug addiction, and a mental health epidemic. These are the global symptoms of escapism of the reality in which we live. We can do so much better, the paradigm must change for a better tomorrow.

Our advances in technology, discoveries in learning, and neurology must revolutionize our systems and how we treat each other. Too long have our minds been segmented by Stone Age dogma, medieval institutions, and 21st century technology that only benefits a few. No more shrinking to fear propaganda for a corrupt state to save us. A synthesis of thought must happen to insure a peaceful world for our children. The approach must be simple, transparent, pragmatic, and above all else fair. It needs to be a streamlined and united in approach to focus the power of the people. Focus on these 7 items, everything else will fall into place.

1. Identify the Parasitical Elements of Society

It's fairly simple to see who are manipulating us for their gain and their own agenda if we care to look. All we need to do is to expose them. The US has been turned into an empire controlled by relatively a small amount of persons (CFR and business cronies) primarily by three methods. These three items need deep investigative journalism, and transparency.

1. Deception.

    Through channels of media propaganda and historical omissions the true motives behind wars and our economic system has been veiled from the general public. The reality of our economic system, and its overall function is never openly discussed in popular media to hide the truth of the robbery of our real production value. This deception leverages our ignorance into fighting wars and agreeing to be more economically shackled by those who think they own us. This is soft slavery folks, and those who are calling the shots fancy themselves our masters.

    The FIX: Demand Transparency. There should be very few secrets in a democratic and open society. The secret files and technology etc. should be open to the public. After all, we are paying for all of it! We should know what we have been paying for all these years. There is no need for such a massive intelligence apparatus, the perceived threats to justify such secrecy do not exist, unless the true threat to power is the American public. For the love of God, let the UFO community know what the government knows. Either way, it'll shut them up or make them really happy if there are any.

2. Economic Leverage

    We need to understand debt has been leverage to exploit us. Creating money out of nothing, and attaching debt to people in the form of compounding interest loans is the name of the game. As a result, we end up giving banking interests our labor and natural resources. If you don't pay back the money created out of nothing, then by government force you are punished. It works the same for the individual as it does for a population. This is the story in the Middle East and Africa. If African's nationalized their natural resources, and the citizens had a stake of ownership in production of their natural resources they would be prosperous. Instead, large multinational corporations take all the profit, and leave the Africans dirt poor while paying off the local politicians. It's just like here, but we still have a better life style. Instead of being exploited as British Colonies, they are exploited by multinational companies being backed by private defense contractors (mercenaries) or the CIA.

3. Military Might
   If people cannot be brought in via economic leverage military force is the next step to subjection. All over the world since World War II, the people associated with the CFR via the US government have toppled government after government as a result killing millions in the name of democracy via intelligence agencies and coup changes. Democracy was the battle cry, the reality was a goal of economic subjection and global hegemony. Close inspection of every conflict and government overthrow shows it has nothing to do with giving a people freedom, and everything to do with control. If freedom was the goal, wouldn't we the originators of said freedom be a lot more free? It's complete bullshit. This is our Foreign Policy dictated by the unelected Council on Foreign Relations.

2. Disband the Centralized Control of the Monetary System and Business Control.

We need to understand the Federal Reserve has turned our country into a nation of debt slaves which has robbed us of our prosperity. We need to understand how fundamental flawed the idea of compounded interest made out of thin air is, and how it relates to human energy as a parasite in economic terms. We need to understand we would be owners, and not living a life of leveraged debtors if we got rid of this system. We need to understand there shouldn't be a middleman involved with every transaction we make as human beings. Alternatives are on the horizon. Like any new idea it takes a bit to get rooted into human consciousness. The internet was once new, and people were skeptical about its value at one time. Look at it now. It has liberated ideas and information like no other time in history.

The underlying technology of digital currencies is what can help decentralize the money cartel. We rely on this middle men to perform as intermediaries in all our transactions, but there is a technology that could render them for the most part useless. This technology is called Blockchain. It holds the most promise in creating a monetary system that is fair. It's not a fiat currency controlled by a group of bankers, but is a cryptocurrency that functions like an asset backed currency. For the first time in human history people everywhere can trust each other to transact peer to peer no matter the distance. Trust isn't established by the corrupt banking industry, but by cryptography and some ingenious coding.

It's interesting how this works. The money, digital asset, are not stored in a central place, but are spread across a global ledger using high level cryptography. Then when a transaction is conducted, it is posted globally across millions of computers. There is a group of tech guys called miners who have a lot of computing power. Every 10 minutes a block gets created that consists of all the transactions for the last 10 minutes. The first miner to validate the block is rewarded in digit currency. Then that block is linked to the previous block which creates a chain of blocks. If you want to hack a block, you are forced to hack all the proceeding blocks in the history of the chain which are heavily encrypted across all the computers globally which store the block chain. In fact, it is much more encrypted and secure than our current monetary system which inherently steals from us. This technology has the ability to replace the financial industries sector, much like the automobile replace horse drawn carriages.

Rather than re-distribution of wealth we could pre-distribute it. We could democratize the way wealth gets created in the first place by engaging more people in the economy. The other great thing about this technology is the inherent privacy. Privacy is the foundation of any free society, unlike the system which exists now where the government without court order can spy on your conversations and banking information. Real production and value creation would be rewarded, not rewarded from passing around manipulated numbers.

Maybe it's time to rethink how business enterprises are owned and ran. Doesn't make sense if all workers of a company owned it, rather than financial firms that squeeze profits from the people working for the firm. If people who work for Ford were stakeholders in Ford they wouldn't be sending jobs to Mexico further eroding American manufacturing. This would also reign in out of control executive compensation packages. In our collective psyche we may want to question a couple assumptions. While it is good to be "rich" and successful it should be that way because you produced something people want. No room for leeches on Wall

Street to take the biggest slice of the pie. Maybe at a certain point, if you are too rich, we should just consider you a greedy dickhead. Hording billions of dollars which represents human energy might not be a good thing. It surely is not in any natural energy system.

Shaming such people might be a good idea, plus its fun to make fun of people who don't think their shit doesn't stink. The trend throughout history is that vast wealth passed down multigenerationally will undoubtedly create a ruling class like we have now. If money has been made our god, we live in a sad society. We might want to start questing the motives of the money clergy, and being more critical. We essentially have a faith based monetary system built upon misunderstandings and lies, lorded over by Banking Class that is more destructive than any pedophile priest. We're all getting screwed.

This system is no longer operating along the lines of rational economic fundamentals, but completely veered into the completely absurd. At a certain point the variance between rational fundamentals and what is going on becomes so large; the divide in the illusion can no longer be hid, faith is destroyed and the system collapses. This is the story of all fiat currencies in history. We are sputtering on the fumes of economic faith, the match is lit, how much longer until this blows up in our face?

3. Return to the Classical Liberal Arts Education System.

We need a return to liberal arts education. In a failing democracy we cannot afford to leave the liberal arts education to the elite. We need it more now than ever before. In a society where we want effective citizens, all people need to have access to the classical liberal arts in order to have knowledge and a moral foundation. This education insures that people think about what is a good life and a good society. It gives the individual skills necessary to conduct a thoughtful life. Today's children need to understand how the human and natural world works. The capacity to evaluate needs to be cultured. These shared values and understanding of rational thought is what built America in the first place. It's required to create a mindful cultural fabric which runs through society. Much like a communications network it connects human beings effectively sharing common morals of the value of liberty, knowledge, and improvement. Out of this collective bandwidth, with the ability to critically think common among most people society flourishes. Currently the network if full of static, distortions, and the bandwidth sucks. We need to upgrade from the current system.

A liberal education is designed to help people seek objective truth, and to use truth to serve society. None of this my truth is as good as your truth bullshit. It promotes thinking citizens, rather than hapless workers. It gives people the ability to question their assumptions, to engage in inquiry to gain new insights about the nature of the world. The liberal arts education our children should be receiving recognizes that the pursuit of knowledge develops our human capabilities and fosters our ability to engage with the world with more depth whether we are working or playing.

Critical thinking, analytical ability, creativity, imagination, and the ability to learn new things is what our modern economy needs, and most of all what society needs. Teach to the test is completely contrary to these needs. One thing China is great at doing is seeing what works and coping it. That's why China is embracing the liberal arts even as we abandon them. The Classical Liberal Arts system of learning information and processing it is a lot like drinking water when you are working out. You can drink a ton of water and not even notice it. When you are focused on tasks, engaged with other people, under low stress the absorption of knowledge is immense. Your working knowledge on subjects become very rich. On the other hand, our stress induced system of forced memorized testing is like shoving a water bottle up your ass, squeezing, and holding it long enough to get to the toilet. You don't absorb much, then after 12 years of school we are still stupid. Then we go to 4 more years of college never being taught how to truly thinking critically. Science and technology guys are taught how to think rationally, but only in terms of their scientific fields. That structural rational type thinking is desperately needed to be applied to society today in a pragmatic way. The devil is in the details, it's about process and technique, and we have it ass backwards from our stated goals.

This recognition would place a huge emphases on the criticality of teachers, and the extremely important role they play in teaching the young minds of this country. This awareness would have ripple effects which positively affect all accepts of society.

4. End Energy Dependence – Empower Each Family.

At the cutting edge of what could be the biggest energy revolution in human history is Elon Musk. What he is pushing for and technologically achieving in solar and battery technology has the ability to fundamentally change energy consumption for every household in World. Another notable person working in this energy arena is Donald Sadoway who is working on an inexpensive, incredibly efficient, three-layered battery using liquid metal.

Elon Musk's company Telsa has built a battery pack called the "Powerwall". The batteries are charged from solar panels on the home, and powers the house when the Sun goes down. This same energy can also power an electric car. This effectively turns your house into its own little power plant. This is energy independence.

Imagine, if this independence was granted to each household where installation is feasible. We could tell the murderous nation of Saudi Arabia to go pound sand! Musk is an example of one of the miracle worker pushing for what many seemed impossible, but is succeeding.

Recently, Musk's company Solar City just released its new solar panels. These panels look just like normal roofing material. The stated goal was to manufacture solar panels that were price comparable to normal roofing material, looked as good or better than normal roofing material, and functioned better than roofing material. Well, they accomplished this goal. This is huge.

A lot of lay people will say, "If it's so good why aren't more people doing it, or why there isn't a bigger push for solar?" Easy, this would completely upset the energy market and place it into the hands of the homeowner. Big companies would make money off the manufacturing, but they wouldn't make profits off residual use from energy such as oil, coal, etc. The people who would be profiting would be local businesses who install, and maintain the systems.

Doesn't it make more sense to catch clean energy directly from the source of all life in our solar system rather than digging up or pumping out back death from millions of years ago then burning it? As somebody who's worked closely with all sorts of electrical systems, and battery systems. It blows my mind this isn't the biggest thing since sliced bread. The deployment of this revolutionary technology is mind blowingly simple. This is the holy grail of energy independence unless somebody comes up with something as clean, but more cost effective. Pour capital into this with the correct people in change, the economic boom would be immense. It would directly benefit people. If you really wanted to see this technology sky rocket into use, team the International Brotherhood of Electrical Workers (IBEW) up with Elon Musk. Resisting this change is like continuing to wash your clothes in a creek instead of using your washing machine. We could stop fracking, we could stop killing brown people in the Middle East, we could maybe start acting like civilized people. Elon, in the off chance you happen to be reading this book please offer me a job. This is a fight worth fighting, our future success as a species depends on this kind of thinking and development.

5. Empower Local Communities and Families.

The establishment power brokers, the people pushing globalization, are the ones causing the global pollution. Then they start talking out of the other side of their mouth about what needs to be done to fix the issue in the form of making carbon taxes. These taxes will be pushed down to the consumer which will further impoverish us. This system of globalization and offshore manufacturing has caused a huge amount of economic and ecological damage when you consider all the materials, parts, and pieces that are crisscrossing the world to find the cheapest exploited labor to use in manufacturing.

The big push by these politicians and corporate global climate change people has little to do with implementing solutions, but to enact more control. Politicians and corporate money people for the most part have very little understanding of technology. The problem is further exasperated by the establishment's propaganda machine called advertising which has manipulate our emotions by subliminally turning our culture into never fulfilled consumers. All of which is built upon leveraged debt, our labor, and our manipulation. If we actually want to fix the problems of global pollution jerking each other off talking about carbon tax, and other such bullshit isn't going to get us anywhere. People, neighbors, and communities need to pull together with developed plans that make sense to become self-sustainable. People with technological know how need to be put in charge of planning and development, not a bunch finance and political know nothings. In order for this to happen, the current debt slavery system must be disbanded. It robs humans of their efficiency.

We need a method for recreating our communities around a central theme of a local food supply and production of local goods. If we are not subject to a debt system as homeowners we are able devote more hours to tasks that sustain and engage the mind and one's creativity. Not being tied to a monthly mortgage payment which demands hours of mindless boredom, slaving away in the corporate culture that really isn't benefiting directly your family or those around you except for the pay check you bring home which is gouged by taxes.

An opportunity to implement a new paradigm is wide open because of the advances in technology. Setting new goals, and making big changes is more tempting than ever because we see the current way of doing this is completely obsolete. It's not working for anyone except for a few rich people. In the deepest recesses of the human mind all we want is to create safety and sovereignty for ourselves and loved ones. We need to put our time and energy into building and living in this new paradigm. Imagine that, working for something we all want and desire. Novel idea.

A sustainable solution to supporting humans in a micro eco-system that is in harmony with the Earth. The technology and methodologies exist, why aren't we doing this? This is called Terraculture. We take care of the planet and ourselves. The thought process is kind of like camping in the wilderness in a sort of way. You tread lightly. If greedy, control hungry people were pushed out of the way this would be easily do-able. Honestly, what large group of people would not be excited about this? Pragmatic achievable goals that will fix society we can collaboratively work on together to offer a better future for our kids is within sight. We are fundamental wired for this sort of thing. It's in our DNA, it's deeply rooted in our minds.

As the emerging science of Neuroeconomics indicates when people work together the brain chemical Oxytocin is released. It is the chemical which binds families, communities, and societies, and fosters trust between strangers. As Dr. Paul J Zak, a Neuroeconomist explains, "oxytocin is primarily a molecule of social connection. It affects every aspect of social and economic life, from who we choose to make investment decisions on our behalf to how much money we donate to charity. Oxytocin tells us when to trust and when to remain wary, when to give and when to hold back." Oxytocin is the love molecule. Our current way of life, our current economic system, and what the media portrays is killing the production of Oxytocin (love) in our minds, and killing our planet.

As technologies in manufacturing evolve more and more work will become automated. Advanced robots will complement or replace workers. As a result, production efficiency will continue to increase along with the advancement in 3D printing. This will provide an opportunity for scale productivity of customized goods on smaller scales at completive prices.

There is a new manufacturing revolution taking place because of the improvements in technology. These technological improvements will make it possible to relocated smaller scale factories back to home markets. Consumer proximity is the new norm because cost of shipping and associated pollution can be drastically scaled back. It would also increase domestic production locally improving the quality of lives communities. The East-to-West flow of trade will end, and trade would be conducted on a regional bases which will lessen pollution. The current model being pushed by the globalists is absolutely insane from an energy use and pollution standpoint; piling up stocks of raw materials, making products crisscross the whole world before they reach their end user. The only way the current model works is leveraging exploited human energy at the expense of the earth's biosphere for profit of a relatively small handful of very rich and powerful people who are in control. By identifying this problem for what it is, and the people propagating this globalist nightmare we can create a cleaner environment, more productivity, and more growth.

Paul Enrlich, an American Biologist concerned with population growth came up with a popular equation human impact on the earth. It's fairly a simple way to mathematically invasion the impact on the Earth with our current system of production and monetary system. Immediately, you'll see T-technology in the numerator increases overall increases the impact.

I=P x A x T

I=Environmental Impact
P=Population
A=Affluence
T=Technology

However, it doesn't have to be that way. T-technology can be moved to the denominator to decrease impact. This is where recycling technologies come into play. It is also consists of leveraging improvements in manufacturing technologies so that production will be localized. This also involves using non fossil fuel energies, and using raw materials that are more easily replenishable.

251

$$I = \frac{P \times A}{T}$$

I=Environmental Impact
P=Population
A=Affluence
T=Technology

We can take this equation further if we really want to think about it more in depth. We need to think about the A=Affluence portion of this equation. We need to factor in the fact we live in debt based system which is hour by hour and day by day forcing more and more production so we can live. Thereby scaling up the impact on the earth just so we can feel secure. We have also been propagandized to the point where the meaning of life has become getting more stuff. Maybe it's time for a new equation that is good for the planet, humanity, and promotes happiness.

$$I = \frac{P \times A}{T \times WT}$$

I=Environmental Impact
P=Population – Maybe have 2 kids instead of 8 maybe a good idea.
A=Affluence - A just monetary system that is not rigid. Buying stupid shit isn't as culturally valued. Remembering experiences in life is all you have when you die.
T=Technology – leverage what we know works, abandon what is hurting us.

252

WT= Working Together – Working together for a common goal that is worth while gives meaning to life. It instills belonging, and Oxytocin.

Families would have the ability to spend more time with each other rather than both parents working all the time, and children being brought up by the dictates of the federal government. Family is at the nucleus of a healthy society, and it's been falling apart for decades. Something is amiss. Meaningful time is what is needed.

6. **Make Some Cool Things.**

We seem to be tapped out on deploying anything that is revolutionary. Things that would make us proud as a nation. We spend billions upon billions dreaming up new ways to kill people, while our infrastructure is going to shit. That doesn't make any sense. Nobody is coming for us, we have some terrorist we created by bombing their lands, and that's about it. Why are we spending so much on defense when we have the ultimate defense? We have enough atomic weapons to kill all life on earth. Can we give it a fucking rest? How fucked up is it spend billions of dollars to create biological weapons to use on other people? This is NO different than the plotting that was done before the "white" man gave the "red" man small pox infected blankets. How about we turn that energy into something helpful rather than destructive. That is pure fucking evil, and we need to hold these psychopaths accountable. Instead of shaming ourselves about the past, we need to fix the present and do great things.

No more wasting money on the insane, and never fully visible. Could we use those resources on something for society? We could build a network of great public transportation that can get people into and out of cities quickly. We could build a network of hyperloop stations which could economically and quickly move people around this country with the fraction of the defense budget.

If we had a moral economic system built upon principles of sound money we wouldn't have to work so much. We could travel, experience life, instead of being a slave to life. This would make tourism a thriving industry which makes everyone happy. Tourism connects the world in a very real way, and gives people the understanding they we are all really the same. We all want to be happy. Sharing the good from cultures is a beautiful thing. In a system of moral economics where exploitation is at a minimum, peace is a natural byproduct.

7. Value Kindness and Being Responsible

Popular media has bombarded us with fear, that being greedy makes you secure, and the state's institutions are the only thing insuring our success and safety. This is the formula of empire. This one is crumbling. Societies built from force, reinforced by greed, and sustained by ignorance ALWAYS fail – and are never happy. Look around, the bricks are falling and the structure is shaking. Higher ideals are lost on the population if they are never reinforced. We are seeing the fruits of this collapse as illustrated in the 2016 Presidential Election between Hillary Clinton and Donald Trump. Welcome to the Republic of Dumbfuckistan.

One civilization in history lasted a long time, Egypt. Are there any clues there? Ancient Egypt of course that their problems like intermarriage, but they accomplished some things that still have

254

people scratching their heads. One of those things is how long it lasted. One reason was economics. It had rich agriculture from the Nile Floods. This gave them an abundance of food that was easily grown, and created an environment self-sufficiency. As a result, they didn't go around attacking people which in the long run would have weaken their society.

This is one place we have gone completely off the rails, this fact was pointed out when Thomas Jefferson stated, "War is an instrument entirely inefficient toward redressing wrong; and multiplies, instead of indemnifying losses." It is a complete resource drain that does not benefit society unless strictly used for defense. Sun Tzu the author of the *Art of War* would think we are crazy. What we are doing only fosters a false sense of security and you create more enemies. A warring society is not going to be an enlightened society. The values needed for civic virtue (social fabric) of freedom and enlightenment are incongruent with focusing on fear, killing people, and being a dick. The same way you cannot say you are a loving parent if you enjoy evoking fear into your children by putting cigarettes out on them.

A few thousand years in evolutionary terms is a drop in a bucket, human being are not much different than the people living back then. Technologies have changed, but the rules of biology, human nature, and how society functions remain the same.

Second item. Sense Egyptians could produce enough food and resources, the people were not forced to endlessly toil. A large segment of the population could focus on intellectual pursuits. Many of the great Greek thinkers went to Egypt to study. When intellectual thought is the focus, and people are not manipulated by fear and greed interesting things happen. A very moral and socially just code of conduct is developed which created a strong social fabric. This code and its importance was emphasized with such importance it reverberated through the culture, and made them successful. This principles were known as the 42 Divine Principles of Maat. Basically, if you live by these principles the result would be a civilized culture of service oriented, honest, and mindful people. As a result, they built wonders we are still scratching our heads about thousands of years later. They had knowledge it took generations to regain. Those monuments and how long the civilization lasted should direct us to the social formula that created that success and start thinking about how we are doing things now.

  We need a society that values the individual no matter race. Where people who have fallen on hard times are not further grinded into the ground, but helped up. Jailing people shouldn't be viewed with vitriol, but should be viewed as human tragedy of epidemic proportions. Empathy is what is needed, a lack of empathy results in societal psychopathy. Examples of societal psychopathy in history are rich: Nazi Germany, Stalin's Russia, and the Inquisitions are just a few examples. It's a scorched earth policy that leads to tyranny and suffering. Underlying tragedies of individuals is deeply rooted helplessness, psychological damage, or neurological issues. Better care, societal empathy, and kindness could cure so many issues we are experiencing today collectively. Fyoder Doskoevsky once said, "The degree of civilization in a society can be judged by entering its prison." Even todays stone casting, so-called Christians, have forgot the words of the one they claim to worship when Jesus said, "Truly, I say to you, as you do it to one of the least of these, you did not do it to me." A country manipulated to and fro by mindless reactionary vitriol of dickheads is turning this place into a sewer of broken dreams and suffering if the prison population is any indication of our success.

At the being of this book the 12 most powerful words in the English Language were brought up: You, Discovery, Easy, Guarantee, Safety, Save, Health, Love, New, Proven, Results, and Free. Is it within human capability to actualize these words in the systems we creates via the voice of reason? I think so, but it will take a shift in thinking that will have to embody these elements in an intellectual way.

If we can wake up to the reality of the situation, apply common sense, and listen to the Voice of Reason this mess can be fixed. Listening to Voice of Reason always leads to HARMONY. Think about the people you know, aren't they pretty much all good people? Don't we all want the best for our children and grandchildren? We cannot let things go any further down this destructive road. Rather than focusing on symptoms of the problems, let focus on the real causes of the problems. When we find absurdities that are controlling or hurting society in a negative way, point them out, and laugh about it. Just like dealing with a bomb, laughter will diffuse the aspects of society which are hurting us. Once these societal bombs are rendered inert, we can get to work dismantling or reengineering what isn't working without fear of an explosion.

Life should be about having fun, smiling, loving those who are close, and respecting others. We can transform our society to something better. We have the tools, the numbers, it will take work, but the biggest problem is in our minds. If we do not take a stand today, there might not be much to stand for tomorrow...

Other Resources:

Korzybski, Alfred. *Science and Sanity: An Introduction to Non-Aristotelian Systems and General Semantics.* 1995.

Chase, Stuart. *Tyranny of Words.* Harvest. 1959

Smith, Homer William. *Man and his Gods.* Little Brown. 1952

If interested, search out work created by these groups:

Zeitgeist

Project Venus

Tragedy and Hope: History so it Doesn't Repeat

www.ingramcontent.com/pod-product-compliance
Lightning Source LLC
Chambersburg PA
CBHW060240290526
45789CB00001B/134